ARE YOU CONSIDERING THERAPY?

ARE YOU CONSIDERING THERAPY?

Anouchka Grose

Routledge
Taylor & Francis Group

LONDON AND NEW YORK

First published 2011 by Karnac Books Ltd.

Published 2018 by Routledge
2 Park Square, Milton Park, Abingdon, Oxon OX14 4RN
711 Third Avenue, New York, NY 10017, USA

*Routledge is an imprint of the Taylor & Francis Group,
an informa business*

British Library Cataloguing in Publication Data

A C.I.P. for this book is available from the British Library

ISBN-13: 9781855758575 (pbk)

Typeset by Vikatan Publishing Solutions (P) Ltd., Chennai,
India

CONTENTS

ABOUT THE AUTHOR

Anouchka Grose is a practising psychoanalyst and member of the Centre for Freudian Analysis and Research, where she regularly gives lectures. She is also the author of two novels, and a non-fiction book, *No More Silly Love Songs: A Realist's Guide to Romance.*

INTRODUCTION

Advising someone to "get some therapy" is easily done. But telling them how, where, and which sort is far more difficult. Should they go via their doctor, follow a friend's recommendation, or try their luck on the Internet? "Therapy" is a word that covers a multitude of different practices. It may involve giving someone a set of techniques to block out unwelcome thoughts, or they may be invited to spend years exploring these thoughts on a weekly, or even daily, basis. In between, there are numerous other possibilities, some of which might include massage, hypnosis, or even dancing. If you're in a difficult situation and have the idea that it would help to go and speak to someone, you may suddenly find yourself confronted by an array of impossible choices and impenetrable terms. Should it matter to you whether a therapist describes themselves as humanistic or integrative? Mightn't it be better just to know whether they are sympathetic and insightful?

If you've decided to "get some therapy", the next step may be trying to work out what that actually means. This book sifts through the more readily available forms of therapy and sketches the main differences between them. While some of these distinctions might look like minor details, others are more glaring. For instance, would you like it all to be over in six weeks? Or does six years sound more like it? Would you prefer to see someone whose aim is to make you feel happy and whole? Or would it be better to work towards accepting your existential loneliness? Not only are people's methods very different, their ideas about "cure" may be diametrically opposed.

Then there's the fact that knowing what kind of therapist a person is isn't enough to tell you whether or not they can help you. No two Jungians or behavioural counsellors are exactly alike. So the other purpose of the book is to say something about the sorts of things you might want to think about when considering psychotherapy—or counselling, or psychoanalysis, or life coaching, or psychiatry, or the many other kinds of treatment on offer. Should you ask to see a prospective counsellor's certificates? Or make judgements based on feelings? Do you have to like your therapist? Or might hating them sometimes form part of the work? And what can you reasonably expect from them?

The field of psychotherapy is not only complex and divided—it can also seem quite obscure. While you may be aware that certain people you know go and speak to someone, they might give very little away about what is actually said. While popular programmes like *The Sopranos* and *In Treatment* are renowned for depicting therapy sessions "realistically", they can't tell you what it would be like to be in therapy yourself. (And both series show only long-term psychodynamic psychotherapy, which isn't necessarily what you'd want to do.) Then there are the peculiar shrinks that pop up in *Austin Powers*, *Meet the Fockers*, *Willy Wonka*, *The*

Stepford Wives, The Silence of the Lambs, Couples' Retreat, and *Analyse That.* If those are the popular representations of therapists, it's amazing that anyone still goes to see them.

You might wonder whether therapy is appropriate for you at all. Perhaps your problems seem too small—or too big. Or even just too weird. This book gives some hints as to the huge range of things that might go on in therapy, both on the side of the client and of the practitioner. There's the question of what people bring, and then the matter of what is done with it. Between those two variables, a lot of different things can happen. It would obviously be impossible to describe what goes on in therapy in one tiny book, but maybe it can help to have some points of orientation before you set off to find out for yourself.

I have tried to be as impartial as possible, but the paradox of a book like this is that, if it's written by someone outside the field, they will be too distant from the subject matter. But if it's written by someone who is immersed in the world of psychotherapy, then they are almost bound to be biased in one way or another. You can't be a shrink without making choices about what sort of shrink you want to be. And while this needn't mean that you think other forms of therapy are rubbish, it probably *ought* to mean that you think your own branch is a particularly good one. So asking a working psychoanalyst to write a book like this is a bit like asking a Muslim or a Buddhist to write a general book about world religions. Still, while it may be problematic, there's no reason to believe they'd do a worse job than an atheist or agnostic. Prejudice can come from anywhere.

On the bright side, I tried quite a number of different treatments before I trained. I've been in one-to-one therapy and psychoanalysis, and have also tried couples' counselling and group therapy. I've had initial consultations with therapists I didn't like, and been on waiting lists that took years to clear. I've certainly used therapy because I felt I needed to, not only out of interest or because it was a requirement for training.

Beginning therapy can be a very brave, frightening, rewarding, desperate, optimistic, difficult, exciting, strange thing to do. This book is an account of the situations and choices you might face if you decide to go ahead with it. I hope it answers a few questions, but I can see that it opens up others. It's more of a start than a finish, but maybe that's better than nothing. If it helps a few people to start something fruitful of their own, I will be extremely pleased.

CHAPTER ONE

What are the different types of therapy?

There are now so many treatments available that it would be extremely hard to compile a comprehensive list. The Wikipedia list of psychotherapies currently stands at close to two hundred, and that doesn't include more alternative treatments that might drop the prefix "psycho" while still considering themselves therapeutic. Some estimates put the figure at around six hundred. In order to keep things contained, I've stuck to the most popular forms of therapy, and skipped anything that involves taking your clothes off and/or pretending to be a lion. Still, this leaves lots of options, from computerized CBT to psychosynthesis (which may involve meditation and screaming). But while the treatments are incredibly varied, studies consistently show that no single style of therapy can claim a better overall success rate than any other. What appears to be true is that different approaches suit different people.

So which approach would suit you? It's probably a good idea to have an approximate answer to this question before you put your foot through anyone's consulting room door. Perhaps you do already. And even if you don't, you may have the broad notion that you'd prefer a short treatment, say, or that you'd hate to see someone who made you do role play. If there are things you know you'd be uncomfortable with, or find stupid, then it's probably as well to avoid them. People's preconceived ideas about whether or not therapy will help them are one of the most decisive factors influencing how much it actually does. If you have the idea that life coaching is superficial or that art therapy is for hippies, then it might be wise to look for help elsewhere. If you think you can feel safe only with someone with a medical background, maybe you'll have to take that as your starting point. On the other hand, you might be utterly repelled by the field of traditional medicine and be drawn to a therapist who would promise to be more sympathetic to your spiritual beliefs. You may be far less interested in their qualifications than in the feeling you get from them when you walk into their room. In the end, you will almost certainly have to choose a therapist using an application of your own bias to the selection of affordable practitioners within reach. This is far from a bad method.

Qualifications

One of the most tangible sets of differences between treatments and practitioners is the nature, and quantity, of their training. In order to call yourself a psychiatrist, you must have completed a medical training and then gone on to specialize in psychiatry. But in order to call yourself a counsellor, you might have done anything between several weeks to several years' worth of training. This isn't to say that psychiatrists are therefore better—or more reliable—than counsellors. Aside from the fact that there are plenty of lazy and unsympathetic psychiatrists in the world, there are also thousands of highly trained and conscientious counsellors. And, perhaps more perplexingly, there are a number of very effective, untrained people who manage to make a great difference to their clients' lives. Just because someone has a certificate, it doesn't necessarily follow that they will be more intelligent or trustworthy than someone who doesn't. A psychiatrist may be great at knowing which drugs produce which side effects, but terrible at dealing sensitively with people who cry. Some are even bad at both. Of course, the newspapers occasionally whip up a bit of a frenzy around the idea of rogue therapists sleeping with their vulnerable clients and running off with their money, but in the overwhelming majority of cases, these practitioners are people with degrees and diplomas who are members of accredited organizations. As with teachers, priests, and medical doctors, the fact that you have passed a few exams doesn't make you a decent human being. Indeed, if you are a proper, forward-thinking evil-doer, a certificate is probably the first thing you equip yourself with in order to get on with exploiting people. Still, it's important to remember that, in therapy as in other professions, the villains make up a very small percentage of the whole.

So I'll try to make sense not only of the myriad treatments, but also to say a bit about the types of training associated with each. But while it may be vaguely interesting to know who has to do what in order to practise under a certain title, it certainly won't be the point to say that people with more training, or experience, are a better bet. The question of what makes someone a good therapist is very hard to answer, and it certainly can't be done by looking at their title or at which certificates they have on their wall. Indeed, I might be quite put off by someone who was too keen to show off their pieces of paper. Wouldn't it be better to actually do some impressive work? Rather than signifying reliability or authority, a cluster of framed certificates might just as well betray a sense of insecurity.

While studies show little difference between the effectiveness of one kind of therapy and another, they do tend to pick out differences in the reported effectiveness of individual practitioners. Within each type of therapy, certain therapists seem to be far more highly thought of than their colleagues. And some of these brilliant therapists are far from the most educated or venerable. In fact, there is some evidence to show that trainees and newly qualified therapists can be more effective than their more established colleagues. But before it starts to look like the best thing to do would be to try to track down one of these super-trainees before they become a jaded old drudge, there are also plenty of reports that state that the most important factor in any treatment is the patient or client. While you have to wonder what sort of research would be able to establish that kind of data, I'm sure any practitioner would agree that a person's expectations and general attitude towards therapy, plus the quality of their life outside it, very plainly influence the course of the work. As a therapist, you can aspire to be as brilliant as you like, but if someone comes to you with the idea that you're useless and won't be able to help them, and that life itself is a horrible thing, it may take an extraordinary stroke of luck or wit to make them think otherwise. Instead of purely focussing on the different kinds of therapy, you might say it's the different kinds of patient or client that you need to be thinking about. There are some people who are inclined to put their ideas and beliefs in question and some who aren't. This distinction may be just as important, if not more so, than the theoretical stance of the practitioner.

While it would be lazy to palm off all the responsibility for what happens onto the client, it's also very important for people on both sides to be very aware of the fact that therapy isn't something that one person does to another, but that it's a relationship between two people. Whatever the practitioner's experience or background, they will ideally be aiming to make it possible for the client to use them as fruitfully as they can.

Still, to simplify things a little bit, you can say that all trainings can be loosely split into two camps. On the one hand, there are therapists who have been taught a series of skills or techniques that can be applied to a patient, while on the other, there are therapists whose training has caused them to ask serious questions about why they are training at all. But in case it sounds like the first lot are taught something useful, while the second lot get caught up in navel-gazing, it's important to bear in mind the importance of *listening* in the therapeutic relationship. One group are taught something like a set of procedures which can be put into action in certain situations, whereas the other people have tried to confront the things in themselves that would lead to preconceived ideas about what another person might need or want. In other words, this second lot have ideally been trained to listen without prejudice (in so far as that is humanly possible).

In reality, it isn't so straightforward. Many trainings aim to combine elements of each—a bit of technique and a bit of self-examination. Perhaps the most concrete thing you can point to would be the division of trainings into those for which the prospective therapist is required to undergo therapy themselves, and those not having this requirement. But even then, there are some courses that require trainees to be in counselling for a few weeks, and others for which they are required to go through *at least* five years of psychoanalysis. If it matters to you what kind of background a person has, you can ask. Even a classical psychoanalyst, who may very well throw many of your direct questions back at you ("Well, what do *you* think?"), should give you a clear answer about the nature of their training, and of the general orientation of their work.

You will ultimately have to make your own mind up about whether you want to work with any particular therapist or not. Some people are good at listening, with or without formal training, and whether their theoretical inclination is directive or more speculative. If you get the sense that the person is really trying to understand and think about what you are saying, then you can take that as a very good sign.

Counselling and psychotherapy

The word "therapist" covers a huge array of practitioners, from self-appointed "nice people" to those with a PhD in Counselling Psychology. The term "therapy" implies someone you can talk to, confidentially, about whatever's bothering you. It's possible to do either long- or short-term therapy. If you see an NHS therapist, it's very likely that you will be offered between six and twelve once-weekly sessions. If you see someone privately, they will almost certainly be more flexible.

The loose idea with therapy is that it's a place to speak about any difficulties you might be having, without *necessarily* having to trawl through your entire psychosexual history. Having said that, this may be the precise thing you need and want to do, in which case your therapist should be prepared to do it with you. And if it turns out that there's more than you can possibly begin to address in six state-funded sessions, they should be able to come up with suggestions for further work.

Ideally, any therapist should be prepared to hear you out and help you think things through on any subject, from trouble at work to a childhood trauma. It's certainly not the case that easy problems are for therapists and hard problems are for clinical psychologists or psychiatrists. The difference is more that therapists are there to respond sensitively to whatever kind of human suffering you bring to them, while a clinical psychologist or psychiatrist, say, would be more likely to make some sort of diagnosis (depression, obsessive-compulsive disorder, borderline personality disorder), and then either treat you accordingly themselves or refer you on to someone else who can.

The things that therapists generally *aren't* thought to be equipped to treat are serious mental disturbances, such as schizophrenia. That doesn't mean that a schizophrenic person shouldn't see a therapist. It just means that a therapist might not feel able single-handedly to treat someone who is floridly psychotic. It may be very useful for someone suffering from delusions or paranoia to have somebody to speak to, but this sort of work would most often be done in conjunction with a psychiatrist (who would be highly likely to prescribe drugs). Still, it might be worth remembering here that therapy is a very strange field. While the general idea may be that it would take a conventional medical practitioner to treat someone with a serious mental illness, in practice this isn't always what happens. Sometimes—even quite often—people manage to get through a manic or psychotic episode without any medication, maybe with the help of the church, or a counsellor, or friends, or a faith healer, or by doing their own writing, or anything else they can come up with that seems to help. So, while a therapist may only be trained to listen and respond—not to prescribe drugs—they may still be extremely helpful in times of serious psychological distress. (However, if they think that a client is a real danger either to themselves or to other people, they may contact the police, the client's GP, or the psychiatric services.)

So, a therapist is someone who hears you out, and who may or may not offer advice. Their responses to what you say will vary according to their personal inclination and/or training; a humanistic therapist is unlikely to be prescriptive, whereas a cognitive therapist may go so far as to give homework.

In the past, there used to be more of a distinction between counselling and psychotherapy. There was a vague idea that counselling was somehow less specialized. This is no longer true. Some clinical psychologists and psychotherapists refer to themselves as counsellors if they think the term makes them sound less intimidating. Apparently, lots of private psychotherapists list themselves as counsellors in phone directories and on websites because they believe that counselling is more commonly sought out than psychotherapy— and because C comes before P in the Yellow Pages. Many courses and training programmes use the title "Counselling and Psychotherapy", meaning that you can take your pick once you've qualified. "Counsellor" certainly no longer implies a practitioner with less formal training than a psychotherapist or psychoanalyst. Someone using this title may have an MA or PhD in counselling and have spent years on the couch themselves. *But* they may also have no formal training whatsoever. You can find out by asking and, if you are at all concerned by their answer, you can ask whether the person is a member of any organizations (such as the United Kingdom Council for Psychotherapy or the British Psychological Society), and then see if you can trace them either through the Internet or over the phone. Because both "counsellor" and "psychotherapist" are legally unprotected words—unlike "Doctor"—anyone can use either title. But not anyone can join an accrediting organization. In order to do this, you have to be a member of a recognized institution (quite often, this will be your training institute), and they have to vouch for you in order for you to be given membership of the larger organization.

This isn't to say, however, that only people who are members of organizations are any good. For a really eloquent argument in favour of independent practitioners, see the movie *The King's Speech* (based on the true story of King George VI's treatment for stammering), which convincingly demonstrates that it's the untrained therapist's empathy, emotional courage, and intuition that make the cure possible. The film also suggests that a state-approved practitioner would have been unlikely to go out on a limb in the way that was necessary to make a difference to the patient; it took a bit of an odd bod to get the job done.

As well as talented amateurs, there are also some highly trained therapists who have ethical objections to the ways these larger accrediting bodies are run. They may be extremely eminent and respected people but, by choice, they aren't on certain official lists of practitioners. If a therapist tells you that this is their position, they ought be able to give you some good reasons as to why. They should also be able to show that their unorthodox position is something they have chosen after serious deliberation.

In the list of treatments that follows, the words "counselling", "therapy", and "psychotherapy" will be used interchangeably.

Art therapy

Art therapy includes music, drama, and dance therapy, as well as visual art. It's quite commonly used in hospitals, schools, rehab clinics, and prisons, although it's also possible to go and see an art therapist privately. Art therapy is thought to be particularly useful for people who find it difficult to put things into words. In sessions—which may take place in groups or one to one—clients are given the materials to make objects or images, or encouraged to move or to act out scenes in the cases of dance and drama therapy.

There are two main ways of thinking about how art therapy works. On the one hand, there is the idea that art-making is in itself therapeutic. If you can express yourself through the things you make, you feel better. On the other hand, there is the notion that art is a medium of communication, so the things you make in a therapy session can be interpreted and offer insights into whatever is going on with you. Art-making may be a way to bypass inhibitions, or to say things that might otherwise prove unsayable. And having got this thing out there, it may then take a trained eye to spot it and to help you to think about what to do about it. This second approach is sometimes called "art psychotherapy". It depends heavily on the interaction with the therapist, on their responses to the things you have made, and your own ideas about what you might be trying to do. In practice, both approaches will often be used together.

In order to become an art therapist, you generally have to have a degree in art, and then to have taken an MA course in art therapy. People working in this field are expected to be quite experienced both as art practitioners and as clinicians. Perhaps because this sort of work is so valued by institutions, it is also highly regulated. Even in the UK, where the legislation around psychotherapy is relatively relaxed, art therapists are obliged to register themselves with the Health Professions Council, alongside paramedics and radiographers.

The idea that art makes you feel better isn't new, but neither is it unarguably true. I heard from one well-known artist that he was offered art therapy after suffering a breakdown and that the very idea made him feel sick. But according to the Freudian notion of "sublimation", art-making could be a way of channelling one's drives and finding a place for ideas or feelings that might otherwise remain totally unaddressed. If you believe that repressed ideas are the force behind symptoms, then it would probably seem very wise to try to deal with them cleverly and not go around acting as though they aren't there. The question is how to go about it. While most therapies put their bets on speech, art therapy tries other channels. One advantage of this may be that most of us use speech all the time, but we don't necessarily paint or dance. If it's so far been impossible to see a way out of our problems, or to understand why we do the things we do, then by switching to an unfamiliar mode of expression, we may do away with habitual thought processes. (This would also explain why art therapy may not be appropriate for artists.) On the down side, some people might feel so embarrassed about their perceived lack of drawing or musical skills that they'd be even *less* likely to be able to express themselves this way than they would in speech. A good therapist may be able to persuade them out of this and to convince them that there's some scope in trying. In the same way that you needn't be a beautiful orator in order to engage in a talking cure, you needn't be a delicate draftsman to get something out of art therapy. It may even be your very inexperience that enables you to use it better.

Behavioural therapy

Behavioural therapy is geared towards spotting "maladaptive" behaviours and correcting them. These could be anything from alcoholism to obsessions or violent outbursts. The point isn't to work on the meanings these behaviours might have for the client, but simply to get rid of the unwanted feelings or activities in order to promote "healthy behaviour". Treatment times aim to be as short as possible—the hope is that people can turn themselves around in the space of a few sessions. Because of this, behavioural therapy is popular with the NHS and with insurance companies.

During treatment, clients might very well be asked to note the things that happen before, during, and after an outbreak of their symptomatic behaviour in order that strategies can be devised to combat repeat performances. Perhaps people will be advised to avoid triggering situations, or given relaxation techniques to use before or during periods of potential upset. The emphasis is on finding tricks that work—thoughts or actions that result in different behaviours.

If someone calls themselves a behavioural counsellor, there is no way of knowing for sure what their training may have involved. The title could cover anything from a self-styled life coach to someone who's done years of research into behaviour modification. If you are at all concerned, you can always ask.

Behaviourists are the group who set most store by scientific research. Indeed, they claim to be quite different to other therapists in this respect. They downplay the importance of the relationship with the counsellor and concentrate more on finding techniques that produce measurable results. Systematic desensitization (exposing the client to the object or event that upsets them) might be an example of this. If a person is afraid of spiders, for example, a behaviourist might try to shift their fear by getting them into the same room as a spider, then encouraging them to look at it, and finally to touch it. If the phobic client can pick the spider up without screaming or fainting, then you have a positive therapeutic outcome. And it's the contact with the spider rather than the contact with the counsellor that counts. This impersonality may be wishful thinking on the part of the behaviourists, however, as a sympathetic or impressive person might have far more chance of achieving a result than someone who is perceived to be cold or lacking in authority. So while behavioural counselling may claim to be the least wishy-washy and most fact-based orientation, it almost certainly relies on the human element much in the same way as do other forms of counselling. You may have to like, or at least respect, your counsellor in order to take their ideas or suggestions seriously.

"Conditioning" is another concept closely associated with behaviourism. There are two types of conditioning, *classical* and *operant*. Classical conditioning refers to the type of trained response made famous by Pavlov and his dribbling dogs: a person (or creature) comes to associate one thing with another because the two appear to be linked. Pavlov's dogs drool at the sound of a bell because, in their experience, the bell is shortly followed by food. A human may associate the sound of a bell with being mistreated because, as a child, the school bell was closely followed by being bullied in the playground. Equally, animals can be taught to associate a bell with being kicked, and humans might learn to associate it with a sense of wellbeing. The point is that living things can be conditioned to link two things so closely that if one of the things happens, it's as if the other has happened—the response is the same. This is a fact used by animal trainers. You can't reward a dolphin with a sardine while it's mid-backflip. But if you can persuade it that a whistling noise is the next best thing to a sardine, then you can whistle while it's flying through the air and give it a sardine after it's landed.

In operant conditioning, a person or animal learns that if they do something they will get a certain result—a cat pushes a lever or a rat runs through a maze in order to be rewarded with food. A human learns, say, that if they smoke a spliff, they are immediately less worried about life. In either case, they may very well keep repeating the action in the hope of achieving the same result.

It's easy to see how both types of conditioning might inform a treatment that aims to get people to behave differently. A symptom is seen as a bad bit of conditioning—a person has unfortunately come to believe that drugs equal happiness, bees equal stings, or that cars equal crashes. So they need to be reconditioned in order to function better. They need either to drop a link between two things (drugs/happiness, bees/stings), or perhaps to forge links between new things (work/happiness, bees/honey).

To give a very extreme example, Anthony Burgess's *A Clockwork Orange* shows conditioning at its most sinister. The anti-hero, Alex, has come to associate classical music with violence. After a spell in prison, he allows himself to be used in an experiment which promises to eliminate his antisocial tendencies. He spends most of a fortnight strapped to a chair with his eyes pinned open, listening to Beethoven while being shown violent films. As he watches, he is injected with a drug that makes him feel extremely sick. It works. At the end of the treatment, he finds himself totally unable to go back to his old ways. Not only does he no longer feel like raping and murdering people, he also can't bear to listen to the music he once loved. The only problem is that he's not happy. He no longer knows what he wants or likes. He hasn't made a moral choice, he has just found himself unable to enjoy the things he used to. This is one of the arguments against the behaviourist approach—while you may get rid of the offending behaviour, you may also leave a hole where the unfortunate activity once stood. And this may very well come to be filled with a new symptom (like Alex's sense of misery and meaninglessness).

Having said all that, you'd be hard pushed to find a behavioural counsellor who'd use the harsh techniques you see in Burgess's novel. For a start, the counselling will almost certainly take the form of a series of conversations. (Eye clips and chemical injections are more the remit of fictional psychiatric experiments, and maybe real-life concentration camps.) It's unlikely, though certainly not unheard of, that a counsellor will take you to the snake house at the zoo, or go up and down in a lift with you. What's far more likely is that they will give you things to try in your own time and then be there for you to report back to. In order to effect reconditioning, they may suggest rewards and punishments you can administer yourself. Perhaps a week without binge-eating can be rewarded with a pedicure, or a day without compulsive hand-washing can prompt a trip to the cinema. Other rewards might come in the form of your counsellor being really pleased for you and congratulating you on your efforts. And punishments might simply be missing out on things you like or witnessing your counsellor's disappointment. When working with children, items such as star charts or sweets might be used to encourage certain behaviours, and the withholding of these rewards would be used as a disincentive.

Because of the emphasis on achieving results, behavioural counsellors will tend to use quite a broad range of tactics, not just the ones typically associated with behaviourism. Desensitization and conditioning may very well appear alongside relaxation and hypnosis, not to mention the less "scientific" techniques of persuasion, encouragement, and suggestion. Good behavioural counsellors will be sensitive to their clients' needs and temperaments, and will adjust their interventions accordingly. This ultimately means that they can't just mechanically apply a treatment to their client, but have to be flexible and intuitive like all other counsellors. So while behaviourism might claim to be the most scientific approach, in practice it is bound to include elements that would be difficult to grasp empirically. According to a study by staunch behaviourists Ullman and Krasner in 1969: "With tact, sensitivity and genuine respect for the person as an individual there is little that is not possible; without these, little can be accomplished." So while behavioural approaches promise quick, visible results, you may still have to track down a counsellor who appears to you to be a decent human being.

Biodynamic therapy

This might also be referred to as "body psychotherapy". Having said earlier that I'd leave out anything that involved taking off your clothes, I've decided to include this one just because stripping off is optional. As well as using speech in sessions, biodynamic therapists may also use massage, as well as art-making and even howling if they think it's necessary.

Biodynamic psychotherapy was developed by the Norwegian psychotherapist and physiotherapist Gerda Boyesen. She was inspired by Wilhelm Reich, the psychoanalyst who became notorious in the 1930s for his use of the "orgone accumulator"—a box in which a patient would sit in order to absorb cosmic energy. Even before the invention of the "sex box", Reich was viewed with some suspicion due to the fact that he touched his patients, who would take sessions in their underwear, and, if things went well, experience "orgasm reflex". While this might all sound a bit outlandish now, it's worth bearing in mind that from ancient times onwards, "hysterical" women were regularly prescribed orgasms by doctors, who would administer the treatment by hand (until the brilliantly practical Victorians freed up the overworked doctors' time with the invention of the clockwork vibrator). There was really nothing particularly new or odd about Reich.

Boyesen thought you had to include the patient's body in the treatment, and to listen to it carefully. She would use a stethoscope to follow the movements of her own and her patients' intestinal tracts during sessions.

She had the idea that the human digestive system wasn't only used to process food, but also to process anxiety, and she called this action "psycho-peristalsis". So, by listening to a patient's insides, you could apparently learn a lot from their gastric responses, plus you could bring about the release of intestinal tensions by massaging other parts of the body, which would in turn affect the psyche. Because of its unique way of attempting to include the body in the treatment, this type of therapy claims to be particularly good at dealing with physical pains and illnesses as well as purely psychological ones. You'd be hard pushed to say how much science is involved in all of this, but that's not really the point. Some people report an incredible sense of relief and feelings of wellbeing after sessions of biodynamic therapy and massage. This may be because Gerda Boyesen was right about the mechanics of the body and mind, or it may be because these clients are very suggestible. It may even be that the two aren't mutually exclusive.

Perhaps one of the strengths of this sort of treatment is its absolute flexibility. It's certainly one of the most free-form of all the established therapies. Not only can you decide whether to keep your clothes on or take them off (biodynamic massage doesn't involve oils, so it's possible to do it through fabric), you can also draw, sing, or do breathing exercises. Given that the therapy is conducted on so many different levels—verbal, visual, physical, even spiritual (if you believe in that sort of thing)—then the relationship with the therapist would be bound to be quite fascinating. It's unusual to be able to deal with another person in such a variety of ways. While biodynamic therapy probably isn't for hard-headed, pragmatic types, it certainly offers a unique and intense mode of interaction with another human being.

Cognitive therapy

As with behavioural therapy, cognitive therapy lends itself to shorter treatment times, typically six to twelve once-weekly sessions. Also similarly, the idea is to tackle a person's fixed ideas without necessarily putting too much stress on where those ideas have come from. As a treatment, it often has a great deal in common with behaviourism, in spite of being quite different in its approach to the human mind. Loosely speaking, behaviourists are more interested in engineering responses—the mechanics of which a person need not necessarily be aware—while cognitivists are more focussed on getting a person to use their conscious mind to bring about change. So behaviourists and cognitivists have sometimes found themselves in disagreement over the notion of "cure". To use the rather extreme example of Burgess's Alex again, a behaviourist might consider him cured when he can no longer perform antisocial acts. But a cognitivist might say he is far from better because he has failed to grasp cognitively the changes that have taken place in him. Alex might want to hit someone, but the very idea brings about an involuntary rush of nausea. It's not until the last chapter (the one erased by the American publisher and dismissed by Stanley Kubrick) that Alex can finally begin to decide for himself that hurting people might be a bad idea. So while the two theoretical standpoints may now be seen to be naturally joined in treatments like cognitive behavioural therapy, there are clear differences between the two approaches.

The word "cognition" comes from the Latin word *cognoscere*, meaning "to become acquainted with" or "to know". Cognitive counsellors go to work on people's "cognitive distortions", that is, the misunderstandings they bring to the world. If someone has the idea that they can't leave the house because a dog will bite them, then they are probably warping reality. They are acting as if they know that a dog will bite them as soon as they step out of the door, whereas it's actually quite unlikely (depending on where they live). So a cognitive counsellor will work with them to shift their distorted "knowledge" and to twist it back into something that better represents a more standardized version of reality.

Bearing in mind the fact that the person's friends and family may have been telling them *for years* that mad, rabid dogs are few and far between, a cognitive counsellor can't simply do the same. Instead, they will use a combination of techniques in the hope that these will cause the person to act differently. Like behaviourists, they may recommend relaxation and breathing exercises that the client can use in stressful situations. When working with phobias, they may use desensitization. There is also likely to be an emphasis on acting differently in order to break destructive habits. Depressed people might be encouraged to make their beds in the morning, or go jogging. But the key idea is to understand how your thoughts and ideas influence the ways in which you perceive the world. Perhaps you don't make your bed because it seems pointless given the fact that you'll only mess it up again a few hours later. But this is also underpinned by your fixed idea that you don't deserve anything nice. Your whole house is a mess because there's no point in cleaning it—why should a scumbag like you have a decent living space? But then you can't ever invite anyone round because it's too shameful, which gives you the sense that you're carrying a big secret, which in turn makes you feel alienated from the people around you, and so on. A cognitive counsellor would try to help you see that the way you perceive yourself is causing you to act in a self-destructive way. They may or may not encourage you to explore why you have such a negative self-image. What they will certainly do is to try to persuade you that it doesn't need to be that way.

As I mentioned before, this type of therapist is very likely to give homework. This may be anything from patting a dog to writing a diary. There's a stress on doing work outside sessions, on putting the counsellor's recommendations into action, and coming back and speaking about how it went. It's a very common-sense approach to therapy. It assumes that people know their symptom is irrational and unnecessary, and so tries to coax them out of it in a semi-supervised way. Clients are expected to be responsible people who want to give up their symptoms because they know that the things they are doing are making them miserable.

There may very well be some discussion of the person's history—maybe they are afraid of birds because they were pecked by a chicken as a child, or perhaps they are chronically jealous because they watched their father cheat on their mother while they were growing up. But these things won't necessarily be questioned and interpreted over time (why did the henpeck seem to *matter* so much?); they will simply stand as the events that set the person's "knowledge" off on the wrong track—just because your father cheated, it doesn't follow that all men cheat. Cognitive therapy tries to access people's automatic responses and make adjustments to them.

If every time you see your partner talking to another woman, you assume that he wants to have sex with her, then this may be a response you feel you have very little control over. A cognitive counsellor might try to establish a few ideas about your situation in order to see whether your automatic responses are in any way justified. If you are afraid of being bitten by a dog and you have indeed been bitten twice by your neighbour's free-roaming Jack Russell, then they might encourage you to speak to your neighbour about controlling their dog. But if there seems to be no concrete reason for you to shut yourself away for fear of an attack, then they will treat your fear as a cognitive malfunction that needs to be adjusted. Similarly for a jealous person—if their partner is a serial philanderer, then perhaps they need to ask why they have chosen to be with that person. But if there are no palpable reasons to suspect them of wandering, then the jealous person needs to give up their false and unhelpful idea and learn to be a bit more trusting. This they will do (in theory) by taking themselves in hand, maybe by breathing deeply or by forbidding themselves to respond in their normal manner to triggering circumstances. Another exercise might involve keeping notes on how your expectations influence situations. Maybe before you go to a party, you already have the idea that your partner will flirt with other people. Perhaps you notice that this is exacerbated by your feeling that your outfit makes you look fat. Maybe you feel competitive with the hostess, or are afraid that everyone hates you since you got a much better job. Whatever it is, you will most likely be encouraged to see that it's your own mindset that leads you to suspect your partner, not anything that they are actually doing themselves.

The bottom line is the idea that there is such a thing as a healthy and correct way of feeling and responding, and that it's possible to train yourself to adapt to it. If, for whatever reason, you find yourself a bit out of whack and doing weird things, then maybe you'd feel a lot better if you pulled yourself together and started being more sensible. A cognitive counsellor will try to help you do that. This is to be a bit flippant about what cognitive counselling might offer, but that's the basic premise. It can certainly be good for people in the middle of a crisis, or people who have a very precise symptom that they want to shift quickly. But it would be a less obvious choice for those who suffer from a more free-floating sense of angst or who want to understand something about why they spent ten years in an abusive relationship—or any other problem of a more mysterious nature.

Cognitive behavioural therapy (CBT) and cognitive analytic therapy (CAT)

CBT, as the name suggests, is a combination of cognitive and behavioural techniques. While the two schools of thought may have had their differences in the past, CBT aims to use elements of each in order to strengthen the effects of the other. Not only will it try to help you understand the ways in which your automatic responses are causing difficulties, it will also give you exercises that you can use to retrain your mind.

Typically, CBT takes place over five to twenty sessions. The first sessions are devoted to mapping out the problem. You may be asked to break it down into its constituent parts: your feelings around it, the behaviours involved in it, the physical sensations associated with it, and any thoughts you may have around it. You will also be invited to describe your current situation. In order to do this, you will possibly be asked to keep a diary. In sessions, all of this information may be taken and organized into some sort of schema or spider graph. Then you and your therapist will go through your ideas and responses and try to establish which of them accurately reflect reality and which are mistaken and unhelpful. Perhaps your low self-esteem leads you to think that people are criticizing you when they are actually trying to help you. Or maybe you drink to overcome feelings of shyness caused by the idea that people won't like you. So you will be asked to put these assumptions of yours in question and to consider the possibility that your perceptions are a bit askew. At the same time, you will devise a set of alternative thoughts and responses with your therapist with which to replace the old, symptomatic ones.

To give an example, a man might turn up saying he's depressed. It transpires that he's in a very difficult relationship and doesn't earn enough money to live. He feels he has nothing to offer the world. Because of this, he tends to get very drunk in social situations in order to block out his own self-critical voices. This leads to hangovers, which lead to him feeling more hopeless and less motivated to work, as well as contributing to rows with his girlfriend. Having established the general layout of his unhappiness, the therapist might encourage the man to see that not everyone values people according to their income, it's being drunk and introverted that actually causes problems when he goes out. Then there's the fact that he has a very good degree and could almost certainly find a more interesting job if he looked for one. But in order to do that, he would need to stop feeling so sure that potential employers would reject him. If he could learn to replace those negative thought processes with positive ones, then he could nip them in the bud before they did any more damage to his life. Being happier in his work and in his social life would almost certainly have an effect on his love life. His girlfriend would no longer have any reason to berate him for being penniless and no fun. So they could either start being nicer to each other, or he could leave her without fearing that no one else would ever find him attractive. These things needn't all happen during the treatment. Having seen what he has to do in order to make his life better, the man doesn't have to keep turning up for therapy every week. He just has to take responsibility for his own actions and to make the necessary changes himself.

CBT is fast becoming the therapy of choice within the NHS, and is also frequently recommended by health insurance companies (far more so than CAT). This is largely due to its brevity, but also thanks to the fact that it endeavours to be empirically testable. Unlike other therapies of uncertain length and outcome, CBT is practised within a set time-frame, setting out to achieve clear objectives specified at the beginning of each treatment. For organizations being asked to hand over money for other people's therapy, it looks like a very good bet. Not only is it short, but it's proven to work. Or at least that's the claim. The only problem with the claim is that the terms of the proof could be said to be slightly questionable. To take the above example, the man may be asked to fill in a questionnaire at the beginning and end of his treatment. In it, he assesses his levels of unhappiness and his general state of mind. If he feels more hopeful at the end than he did at the beginning, then the treatment is judged a success. He may very well feel quite optimistic at the end, because he has been given a personal action plan that tells him exactly what he needs to do in order to feel better. The problem is that no one knows what the man will *actually* do next—not even the man himself. Just because he has been given a set of strategies for making his life good, it doesn't necessarily follow that he will use them. Still, if he doesn't, he will at least know it's his fault. So if CBT doesn't help him, the problem isn't with CBT, it's with him.

This is why CBT is so often criticized by therapists whose work is more open-ended and less goal-driven. For them, this sort of therapy fails to take human complexity into account. It gives people the false idea that if they are sensible, work hard, and do the socially acceptable thing, then they will live happily ever after. It certainly doesn't consider the possibility that it's often the fact that people are trying so hard to shoehorn themselves into a standardized version of "normality" that makes them depressed or anxious in the first place—as the person-centred therapists have so sagely pointed out. CBT also gets people's backs up when it claims to be a "better" treatment than others due to its apparent empiricism. You really can't generalize about what an individual might need, so it's not wise to make broad claims about what works in therapy and what doesn't. But the thing that makes their claims of superiority really inflammatory is that they are connected with money. CBT has been developed in such a way that it fits perfectly within an audit culture that wants to see quick results delivered at minimum cost. Governments and private insurance companies are bound to smile on a treatment that explicitly offers value for money, so it has quickly achieved a dominance that may not be justified by its long-term effects.

In response to this, an advocate of CBT might say that they are simply trying to give people the tools to live better. Just because people with more humanist or psychodynamic leanings don't make such clear promises, it doesn't follow that they can actually help you more. It just follows that it can be hard to know precisely what they're offering you. And it also follows that you can't put their work to the test.

For someone outside the field who just wants to get some help, this sort of squabbling between different factions may seem like a mystifying waste of time. And if they're supposedly so sorted, why do they argue so much? With all that going on, how can anyone hope to put their faith in a single therapist and get some work done? As ever, you are left to fall back on your own intuition. If you are a fiercely practical person who has little time for the past, then CBT may very well seem like the obvious choice.

Cognitive analytic therapy is a relatively new type of therapy, developed in the 1980s by a GP and psychotherapist called Anthony Ryle. It was specifically designed for use within the NHS, where funds are scarce. It attempts to combine the speed and functionality of cognitive therapy with the depth of psychoanalytic approaches. Treatments usually last for around sixteen sessions. Cognitive analytic therapy uses some of the same techniques as cognitive behavioural therapy (CBT)—diagrams, homework, strategies for dealing with maladaptive patterns—but also pays attention to the relationship with the therapist and considers this a serious aspect of the work. The psychoanalytic component mainly takes ideas from object relations theory (which I'll discuss more fully in the section on Kleinian psychoanalysis). Put a little over-simply, this means focussing on the earliest stages of human development and seeing how our very first interactions with our carers inform everything that happens afterwards. It also involves looking at the ways in which the relationship with the therapist echoes these early relationships. Maybe you fear your therapist's rejection so you don't want to tell them anything bad about yourself. Or perhaps you're always late because you want to show them you don't need them. This sort of revealing behaviour will be interpreted back to you by the therapist.

In CAT, a client is encouraged to see how their current problems are partly informed by experiences in their distant past, and how the tricks they've developed for dealing with their difficulties may actually be making things worse. One of the special features of CAT is that, after the first few sessions, the therapist presents the client with a "written reformulation"—a piece of writing laying out the ways in which the therapist believes the client's history is impacting on their present. This information will also be laid out in graphic form. The client's symptoms, or the things that make them unhappy, will be listed in this context as "target problem procedures", which need to be dealt with differently in future.

So, quite early on in the treatment, you are given a clear indication of what your therapist thinks of you. From here, the sessions become much less structured— you can discuss the ideas that have been presented to you in whichever ways you like. But the basic aim will be to develop a better understanding of your situation and to take responsibility for dealing with it. Towards the end of the treatment, there's a kind of summing up. While you won't be expected to have made all the necessary changes in such a short space of time, you *will* be expected to have a good idea of what they ought to be. CAT tries not to foster a dependency on the therapist, but to set the client up to deal with their problems by themselves. The treatment finishes with an exchange of goodbye letters between client and therapist, where both sides say what they think has been achieved in the therapy. After this, it's quite common to have one more follow-up session a few months later. This style of therapy is often described by its proponents as being safe, user-friendly, and evidence-based. By aiming to be both quick and functional as well as deep and complex, it hopes to answer the standard objections to therapy from both ends of the spectrum. For the people who complain that much therapy is unwieldy and erratic, CAT offers a sensible programme for bringing about change. And for people who suspect brief therapies of being superficial, CAT practitioners claim to offer a space for clients to explore their unconscious motivations within a psychotherapeutic setting. This is a laudable aim, and you can see why it might appeal both to people seeking therapy and the organizations that fund it. In a sense, you can't lose because all bases are covered. It's surely the best form of therapy ever invented. The only question is whether these aims are achieved—or whether they may actually be mutually exclusive. If the framework really is as safe and as tried and tested as it claims to be, then how can it also contain the possibilities of opening up the unconscious and of tackling the psychodynamics of a relationship with another human being? Both processes are extremely unpredictable. To say that they can be dealt with inside a predetermined timescale may be rather naïve.

If you wanted to be harsh, you could say that CAT practitioners prefer to blind themselves to the illogicality of their offer simply because it would be so nice if it were true. But, to be more generous, you could also say that, by being a bit Pollyannaish, they make therapy available to a wider group of people. If treatments like CAT manage to convince governments and insurers that talking cures can offer a good return on their investment, then people who might not otherwise be able to afford therapy will have access to it. While they may not *actually* be getting a "better" and more "proven" kind of treatment than any other, the fact that the funding bodies believe they are at least means that there can continue to be a mainstream alternative to the blanket prescription of cheap and cheerful drugs like Prozac. Although independent studies might show that more "alternative" treatments, like biodynamics, are just as good as CAT, it's unlikely that nervous bureaucrats would dare to invest in something that looks so wild on paper.

Computerized CBT

Because CBT isn't overtly reliant on the relation between client and therapist, then there is a school of thought that says you can do away with the therapist altogether. You can replace an expensive live human with a cheap CD-ROM. This isn't such a strange idea—it's the basic premise of most self-help books, after all. If you have a therapy that doesn't rely on the murky and mysterious interaction between humans, but depends instead on practical solutions, then it should work just as well on paper or online as it does in a consulting room. There are plenty of CDs, books, and websites that offer some kind of DIY CBT. In the UK, there is a CD called *Beating the Blues* that is given away by the NHS to people suffering from anxiety and depression. On it, you'll find eight "sessions" that you can go away and do at home. The course of the treatment follows the same basic shape as live CBT—the initial session suggests that you outline exactly what your problem is. It also gives you homework to do in the week before your next session. The following sessions take you through everything from "activity scheduling" and "problem solving" to correcting "thinking errors"—and distraction techniques you can use to stop yourself thinking unhelpful thoughts. It's not exactly considered to be a replacement for drugs or therapy—it's often given to people alongside tablets, or when waiting lists for flesh-and-blood therapists are too long. Apparently some people like it because it spares them the embarrassment of exposing their problems to another human being. It may even make it possible for very shy, inhibited people to try out a kind of treatment that would otherwise be out of the question. (Of course, you might say that they are precisely the people who need to see a live shrink, but they may not agree with you.) On the down side, people often object to being offered a cheap, quick fix when they have turned up hoping to find someone to speak to about their extremely upsetting problems. For them, computerized CBT is just simplistic, inhuman, and insulting.

"Cure" is one of the strangest ideas in therapy because it's so slippery. Anyone who is analytically minded would be inclined to suspect sudden, drastic improvements. Freud came up with the notion of a "flight into health" whereby a person might hastily drop a symptom in order to avoid psychoanalysis. They might do this at a moment when they sense that shameful material is about to emerge. Rather than risk being exposed in front of their analyst—and maybe being encouraged to give up an unconscious enjoyment—they can hastily claim to be cured and stop coming. This sort of thinking is used against psychoanalysts by more pragmatic thinkers who see it as a way of continuing to extract money from patients when they no longer need to come; if they don't have their symptom, then they don't need their shrink. But if you accept the idea that people may avoid an encounter with a real person because it risks being too revealing, then you can see how computerized CBT, and the reading of self-help books in place of therapy, might be a way of running away from something rather than addressing it; you can appear to be thinking about your problems while studiously avoiding them. But then again, of course, a shrink *would* say that ...

Existential psychotherapy

This form of therapy is almost diametrically opposed to CAT, CBT, SFBT (solution-focussed brief therapy), or any other kind of treatment whose passion for brevity might lead to its use of an acronym as a name. Existentialists would never claim to offer some kind of "evidence-based" cure because, for them, the overwhelming evidence is that there *is* no cure for the human condition. Based on the ideas of Kierkegaard and Nietzsche, existential psychotherapy aims to see people through the anxiety of realizing that there is no God, we're all going to die, we have the freedom to at least try to do whatever we like, and we are fundamentally alone. While other therapies might be accused of hoodwinking people into imagining that life can be great if you just pull yourself together, existentialism encourages people to get real about the fact that life can be pretty terrifying and there's no reason to believe in happy endings. Still, it's not necessarily a fast track to misery. Being realistic about the facts of life might enable you to find ingenious ways of dealing with them.

According to this way of thinking, some other therapies might be accused of presenting people with a fictional idea of what it means to be "well". Encouraging people to believe that their partner really loves them, their employer wants the best for them, and that the world in general is a kindly environment could be said to be a cruel trick. If you tell people that it's only their naughty, maladaptive patterns that are making them unhappy, then you are perhaps encouraging them to buy into a comforting illusion about the kind of planet they are living on. While it might be possible to go along with this sort of chirpy notion of mental health for a short while, there's a distinct chance that events may chip away at it. While you go around with the fixed idea that things are "all good", they may reveal themselves to be a bit more ambiguous.

Existential psychotherapy would try to help you deal with this sort of ambiguity, and to be prepared for it. By being alert to the painful limits of existence, you can find more spirited ways of dealing with them than by simply blocking them out, or by feeling defeated. Existential therapists won't have any set programme for helping you to do this. There certainly won't be diagrams or "written reformulations". The therapist will simply try to help you see how your suffering is a response to the four universal problems of death, choice, isolation, and meaninglessness. What you do about it is your business. Maybe you decide that suffering is just part of life, and so you get on with enjoying the good bits and putting up with the bad bits. Maybe you decide that you really do want to be an opera singer more than an office worker, even if that means risking failure. Perhaps you decide to leave your wife and kids and run off with your secretary, losing the sympathy of all your friends and family in the process. But if it's what you really feel you have to do, then your therapist should be able to see you through it, to understand something about why it's so important to you, and to help you to bear the consequences.

Not only is there no fixed idea of cure, nor of how the treatment should unfold, there's also no firm notion of what an existential therapist should be like. Each practitioner would be encouraged by their training to find their own ways of working, and then to adapt them in turn to each patient. Every individual therapist's own thoughts on coping with the pain of existence would inform their practice. Their "style" would come out of the solutions they have developed in their own therapies and in their lives. This would presumably mean that, if you think that this sort of therapy might suit you, it may still be wise to look before you leap and to find someone with whom you feel you have a good rapport. Unlike, say, CBT, which tries to homogenize the treatment procedure to the point where it can be administered by a CD-ROM, existential therapy may be very different in each case. So while there are four basic problems that we all have to cope with, there is a multitude of existential therapists, each with different ideas about how to come at them.

Gestalt therapy

This type of therapy has a lot in common with the existential kind. It encourages people to think about their problems in the context of the world in which they live, and to take responsibility for their lives. The word *Gestalt* means "shape" or "form" in German, but in English it has come to mean something more like "the whole thing". So a gestalt therapist tries to get an idea of the shape of the whole picture. Gestalt therapy takes everything into account, from the person's childhood to the relationships they have with their friends and family, their work, their culture and religious background, and, very importantly, the way they deal with their therapist. It also entails paying attention to one's feelings in the present. In gestalt therapy, you will be invited to speak a great deal about what's actually happening to you *right now*. Perhaps that thing you just said made you feel anxious. Maybe you have a strange sensation in your left leg. Or you are desperate to see your therapist smile. By articulating these emotions or sensations, you may not only become more attentive to them, but you start to see them in the context of your relationship with another person. It's possible that you think your therapist *makes* you feel a certain way. Or that they can, or should, help you. Gestalt therapy is very focussed on *relationships*—you and your therapist, you and your father, you and the world at large.

Often, a gestalt therapist will focus less on what the person is saying than the way in which they are saying it. Do they mess around apologizing before they speak? Explain dogmatically? Smile and giggle while discussing unpleasant things? The client's tricks and strategies for dealing with another person will be brought into focus. The therapist will help the client see how their ways of interacting provide an insight into their psyche. Are they placating the other person? Trying to entertain them? Shutting down in the face of their imagined hostility? Whatever it is, it will become a focus for discussion and interpretation as much as—if not more than—the content of the person's speech.

Perhaps the best-known aspect of gestalt therapy is its use of the "empty chair technique" (also known as the "open chair technique"). The therapist will keep an extra chair in the room for this purpose. The client will be told to imagine that a significant person is sitting in the chair—perhaps their mother or father, or their annoying neighbour. They will then address the person as if they were actually there. They will be encouraged to really express their true thoughts and feelings, not to hold back as they do in real life. Then they will often be asked to sit in the chair and to answer themselves back from the point of view of the imaginary third party. In this way, they will not only vent their spleen, but they will also have a chance to empathize with the other person. Gestalt therapy is thought to be good for people who are uptight and find it hard to express their real feelings. It gives them a chance to let them out and then to think about how reasonable or unreasonable they might be. Not all gestalt therapists will necessarily use this technique—like the existentialists, they are more interested in making way for authentic interactions than in following any kind of rulebook.

Gestalt therapy was developed throughout the 1940s and 1950s by Laura and Fritz Perls, two German psychotherapists, who were later joined by the American writer Paul Goodman. They took influences from all over the place, not just the world of psychoanalysis and psychotherapy, but also from systems theory, contemporary theatre, and Buddhism. Having escaped the Nazi regime, Laura and Fritz Perls arrived in New York, via South Africa, where they set up the first gestalt institute in their house. Their work became incredibly influential during the 1960s and 1970s, so much so that it almost seems to define a generation. The idea that therapy involves getting in touch with your feelings and letting it all hang out is very gestalt, as is the idea of doing your thing and letting other people do theirs. This is the main point of Fritz Perls's famous "Gestalt Prayer", which he wrote in 1969, and which has since been made into posters and displayed in wholefood shops and yoga centres all over the world.

Gestalt therapy is far less popular than it used to be, perhaps because the dominant therapy culture has shifted away from letting it all hang out, and towards packing it all back in. It's interesting, though, that Eastern philosophy has been a big influence on both. While the older way of thinking plays up the "live and let live" approach of Buddhism, the newer kinds of therapy are especially interested in Eastern techniques for controlling extremes of feeling—meditation, self-persuasion, and the general message that excesses of emotion aren't good.

Humanistic counselling

This may also be called person-centred, client-centred, or Rogerian counselling (after Carl Rogers, one of the original 1950s humanists, alongside Abraham Maslow). If behavioural and cognitive counselling fall on one side of a line, then humanistic and psychodynamic counselling could be said to fall on the other. While the first two approaches aim to clear up symptoms as swiftly and efficiently as possible, the second two are all about giving a person the opportunity to explore ideas and feelings in the context of a relationship with another human being. And, like the first pair of approaches, these two are also subtly different from one another.

In humanistic counselling, great importance is placed on a good connection between therapist and client. Indeed, it's the relationship itself that's seen to have healing properties. A humanistic counsellor certainly can't sit in silence and wait to see what their client comes out with—they must demonstrate that they truly want the best for them. If the client suspects that the counsellor is faking or only doing it for the money, then this would be a sure sign that things aren't going to plan. So a counsellor of this sort must either have a genuine love and respect for their fellow beings, or be an *extremely* good actor.

A humanistic counsellor would never refer to the people they work with as "patients" but as "clients". A "patient" would seem to them to imply a sick person coming to see an expert, whereas the use of the word "client" aims to give the impression of someone who comes along to use a service of their own free will. Humanistic counselling aims to be non-hierarchical— the counsellor and the client are simply two human beings trying to work something out together. The counsellor may very well tell stories or use examples from their own life if they think these may be rele- vant to the client. This makes it different from the psy- chodynamic approach, in which a person's ideas and fantasies about their counsellor may form an impor- tant part of the treatment—if the counsellor gives too much away about themselves, then these imaginings risk being curtailed.

The ideas that Rogers, Maslow, and colleagues devel- oped had their roots in existentialism, albeit a rather more cheerful version than you'll find in Camus or Sar- tre. For humanist therapists, all people have the capac- ity to reach their full potential (to "self-actualize") and live happily. The problem is that most of our experi- ences have led us to limit ourselves or bend ourselves out of shape in order to please other people. Because it's so important for humans to be loved, we will do almost anything in order to make it happen. So human children may try to please others by keeping quiet, not making demands, or by acting in any way that they believe will ensure affection from the significant peo- ple in their surroundings. They may even be noisy and demanding if it seems to them to generate a bet- ter response. Perhaps sometimes they'll get it wrong and be punished. Maybe they'll be pushed aside by a competitor. And perhaps they'll be unlucky enough to be born into a situation where there's very little love available whatever they do. This may well cause them to grow up believing that it's them, not their surroundings, that are at fault.

A humanist will take as a given the idea that each person is intrinsically loveable. By truly being there for their client, listening non-judgementally, and giving guidance and encouragement, they will hope to undo whatever damage has been done. In this way, the client will stop doing foolish and self-defeating things and get on with being freer, more creative, and much more cheerful. Humanists have a high opinion of people in general. While a Freudian may see civilization as the miraculous outcome of the fierce suppression of our intrinsic destructiveness, a Rogerian would be more inclined to believe that people are fundamentally good, and that it's only the contingent bad things that happen to them that set them off on the wrong track.

It's the very "niceness" of humanist thinking that sometimes generates criticism. It isn't simply the fact that humanists have a rosy view of human nature. For certain clinicians, the problem with this approach is in the fact that the counsellor themselves is so nice to the client. In the face of so much warmth and understanding, it may become difficult for the client to express their own darker, more unsavoury feelings; it may prove too shameful to expose your own horribleness in front of someone so sweet. The humanist counterargument to this is to say that a good counsellor would be sufficiently skilled and tactful to make it possible for their client to say whatever they need to say. The counsellor themselves may choose to speak about their own experiences of anger and hostility if they feel it might open things up for the other person. The point isn't to be "nice" in the normal sense of being polite and slightly artificial, but to be authentic. This would necessarily involve having a realistic take on your own capacity for "nastiness".

In terms of training, there may be a bit of a paradox. You could say that it's very important for a humanist counsellor to have dealt properly with any problems they might have in the field of human relationships. If they're going to commit themselves to being there for other people, really and truly, then they'd better have done something about their own ambivalences and intolerances. What if someone turns up who tests their capacity for open-mindedness: a paedophile, a racist, a misogynist—or just someone who reminds them of their despised older brother? Will they turn them away? Tell them that they disapprove of their ideas or actions? Or trust their love of humanity to overcome all evils? If they have been through counselling themselves—or if they just happen to have been born perfect—then they may very well be able to cope with all sorts of testing situations. But this would suggest a special, highly trained, or highly gifted individual, not just another person muddling through life. But because humanists insist on the symmetry between client and counsellor, then the idea of a specialist is an anathema.

This leads to practices such as co-counselling, where two "clients" counsel one another and there isn't a therapist in sight. The advantage of this is that it's free for both parties. (This also makes quite certain that the other person isn't simply in it for the money.) Another advantage of co-counselling may be that some people feel more comfortable speaking to an equal than an expert. The disadvantages are so obvious that I hardly need list them: you have to take all the other person's problems into account as well as your own, you may feel very responsible for them, you may wonder what help you can hope to get from someone who hasn't found a way through the problem themselves, you may compete to be "healthier" or "sicker" than the other person, and you may wonder why on earth you aren't just speaking to your friends.

Humanistic counselling would probably be a good choice for people who aren't in a big rush to drop a very concrete symptom, but who feel they could do with speaking to a sympathetic person about whatever happens to be troubling them at the moment. It can either be a long- or a short-term arrangement. The length would depend on a number of factors. An NHS counsellor would generally tend to offer a shorter course of six to twelve sessions, whereas a private counsellor would almost certainly be more flexible. In private treatment, you should be able to attend for as long as it seems to the two of you to be useful.

Integrative psychotherapy

Here the title refers both to the person in therapy and to the theoretical framework of the work itself. The idea is to integrate ideas from all sorts of different therapies in order to help a client achieve a sense of integration. It claims to be different to "eclectic therapy" in that it doesn't just involve the therapist doing a bit of this and that according to their whim but, like CBT, is built on a well-researched set of ideas about what actually works. If each different kind of therapy is the outcome of a person or group of people deciding to practise in a new way, then integrative therapists try to have an overview of all these idiosyncratic ways of working. Integrative psychotherapy relies heavily on cognitive and behavioural approaches, but it aims to go deeper than brief therapies. While it's important to know what achieves results, the goal isn't to patch things up so they look OK, but to really help the person explore the material they bring.

An integrative therapist would be trained to be suspicious of sudden, miraculous improvements. If after three sessions, a person comes in and says, "I've stopped binge-eating and I really love my husband again", there's a chance they may be trying to please their therapist and/or to show them that they don't need them any more. So, without being churlish, it may be wise to question this sort of magical effect.

The general drift of this type of therapy is to get the person somehow back in synch with themselves and to give them the sense that all their parts fit together. If they are falling back on strange coping mechanisms developed in childhood, while at the same time holding down a job with huge responsibilities, there might be the idea that they need to catch up with themselves a bit. By gaining some insight into their unsettling behaviours, they could gradually give them up and start acting more in keeping with the healthier parts of themselves. In other words, therapists of this sort believe very much in the possibility of a healthy whole, but they know that the psyche is complicated and they don't imagine you can sort it all out in five minutes.

It's another of those therapies that aims to be reasonably watertight. They've weeded out all the wacky parts from the array of therapeutic options and are left with only the excellent bits. But maybe it's not that simple. They also say that they don't go in for a one-size-fits-all approach. What works for one person is wrong for another. So they apparently know, in a properly well-researched way, what will be best for each individual. There's no guesswork in it, it's the result of serious studies. (Of every individual in the world?)

Of course, it's unfair to be offhand about a group of therapists who are no better or worse than any other, but it seems as well to be wise about what's being offered. If all therapies are basically conversations with another person, then what marks them out from other forms of conversation? If the premise is that your co-conversationalist has been trained to really know what's best for other human beings, then maybe it's time to worry. While individual practitioners in this field may be excellent, there is something in the theoretical claims of this branch of therapy to which some people might take exception. While at first glance, it may seem like a good idea to take all the provably best bits from all the therapies and pack them together, at second glance it can start to look a bit woolly. Or even authoritarian. No therapist can ever *know* what's best for you. They can only ever try to help you work it out for yourself.

As ever, if you go to meet someone of this orientation with a view to starting therapy, all you can do is see how it goes. If they are easy enough to talk to, ask good questions, seem wise, have nice carpets (or whatever else you feel gives you clues as to whether they can help you), then by all means go ahead. Lots of therapists—maybe even most—choose their trainings without really knowing the full implications of the theory that backs up their work. Maybe they chose their training institute because it was nearest their house, or what they could afford, or the one their friend recommended. It's only by living with the theory and learning about other theories, and seeing how the theory relates to live, troubled individuals, that you can even begin to understand what it all means. Having trained as one thing, you might begin to see the advantages of a different approach. Every practitioner will read and respond to theory in a different way—and will then have to face the fact that theoretical knowledge can't make you a good shrink. Or even that there's no such thing as a good shrink—one client gets better, another gets worse, one hates you, one loves you. There is no best possible form of treatment. So just because someone has trained under an orientation whose claims are problematic, it doesn't at all follow that they are a bad bet.

Person-centred psychotherapy

This one has an especially good title. It helps people to distinguish it from lamppost-centred psychotherapy, or muffin-centred psychotherapy, and all those other ones that you might risk confusing it with. Person-centred therapy is really, really lovely. (See the section on humanistic counselling—it's based on the same ideas.) The therapist genuinely cares about the client, the client feels nurtured by the relationship. It's all real, nobody's putting on an act. The therapist talks about him- or herself. There's no hierarchy. Except that when it starts to be called "psychotherapy" or "counselling" rather than "a nice chat", there's probably an implication that the practitioner is a fully trained, serious professional. Still, perhaps it really is possible to get over this stupid, bureaucratic fact. Yes, they may be a member of an accrediting organization, but that doesn't stop them being a human being. Perhaps the most excellent thing about this kind of psychotherapy is that it accentuates the strangeness of the therapeutic promise. On the one hand, the person is a professional, but on the other hand, they are just another flawed creature like you.

In Rogerian/person-centred psychotherapy, the well-trained and policed automaton side of the therapist is played down and the "person" side is played up. But what if they really were *very* flawed? Then maybe they wouldn't make it through the process of becoming a registered, person-centred psychotherapist. So they have to be a thoroughly decent and loving person. But will this be thanks to their therapy and their training? Or will it be because person-centred training institutes know how to pick out the naturally nice people, and then the training is just a formality? Or are they right in saying that all people are good if they can only allow themselves to be?

As ever, if you find a good one, don't let the paradoxical premise put you off.

Psychodynamic psychotherapy

This type of therapy is the nearest to traditional psychoanalysis. It takes the idea of the unconscious into account and doesn't assume that we are completely rational beings, able to change at will. Perhaps we get some hidden satisfaction from the things we claim to be upset by. Or maybe the forces underpinning our troubling feelings, thoughts, or actions are so powerful that we can't simply override them and expect them to go away. A psychodynamic therapist will encourage you to explore the ways in which your current situation is informed by your past—particularly by the coping mechanisms learned in your childhood.

Psychodynamic counselling is underpinned by child development theory, and by the idea that the problems you run into—and the solutions you find—at certain moments in your early childhood will inform the sort of person you become. These ideas are so much a part of popular culture now that they're often used without any serious consideration of what they might actually mean. It would be normal sitcom-speak to refer to someone as being "very anal", for instance. What this means, technically speaking, is that the person is uptight because there was a difficulty that they encountered during potty training, which they resolved by withholding bowel movements. (For some reason, it's the neat, controlling "anal retentives" rather than the messy, chaotic "anal expulsives" who seem to have the monopoly on popular consciousness.) While this *may* be the sort of thing you talk about with a counsellor of this type, it might not be totally necessary to go quite *so* far back. As opposed to a classical psychoanalysis, where no association is too obscure, no quasi-memory too uncertain, psychodynamic counselling offers a space to make links between your past and your present without necessarily dredging through the whole lot. There might be a particular problem you want to deal with, without having to speak about *everything*. You won't usually be asked to lie on a couch, and while you will be invited to speak freely and openly, you are unlikely to be asked to free-associate (to say whatever comes into your mind, without editing).

Another feature that marks out psychodynamic counsellors is their use of the transference in the work. "Transference" refers to the feelings the patient or client has towards the therapist. Because the therapist is quiet and doesn't give too much away—and also because they are in the place of a knowledgeable person who takes care of the client—the client is very likely to project certain ideas onto them, informed by their own prior experiences. The therapist might be seen as a parent figure, friend, or sibling. This is called "transference" in order to emphasize the fact that whatever feelings the client has about the therapist are bound to have been transferred over from someone (or a few people) in their past. The client doesn't actually *know* the therapist, but may nonetheless find themselves having quite strong feelings about them—both positive and negative. Maybe they are desperate to please or entertain them, maybe they always disagree and try to prove them wrong, perhaps they are constantly asking for little favours—a letter, a glass of water, they want to borrow a book. The counsellor will take this sort of thing as seriously as anything else the client says or does. The client's expectations and projections may give huge clues as to the ideas they have about people in general, which will in turn have been informed by significant figures in their life. So by asking questions and trying to find out about a client's personal history, and by simultaneously observing the ways in which they act in the present, the counsellor will hope to piece something together about the way the client's past is impinging on their life. Perhaps their absent and self-absorbed mother has left them desperate to extract love and special attention from women—hence their insistence on demanding extra help from their female counsellor. (They want to pay a reduced fee and dry their socks on the radiator during sessions.) Perhaps the unchecked competitiveness between the men in their family makes it difficult for them to expose any vulnerability in front of their male therapist.

Psychodynamic counselling is insight-based, which makes it very different from behavioural counselling, where the emphasis is on acting differently *not* on knowing what makes you act that way in the first place. So a psychodynamic counsellor will be unlikely to expect you to draw diagrams of your behaviour patterns or to suggest certain courses of action. The idea is just to help you think about why you do the things you do in the hope that your greater understanding will open the way for you to do them differently.

The main criticisms of this type of counselling come from two completely different directions. People who are more inclined towards the behavioural model might say that the psychodynamic approach is slow and imprecise and doesn't offer much in the way of practical help. And people who are more psychoanalytically oriented might say that it's nonsense to imagine you can single out one bothersome aspect of your life and not worry about the rest of it. They might see this kind of counselling as psychoanalysis-lite—an approach that pays lip-service to the unconscious without actually taking it seriously. That's all very well, but not everyone wants to commit to lying on a couch five days a week for fourteen years. So psychodynamic counselling might be a very good place to look into a particular problem in a non-directive way, and to explore something about what makes you *you*, without being told what to do, or made to feel like you ought to be different. As with humanistic counselling, there is no recommended number of sessions—the length of the treatment can be decided between you and your counsellor.

Psychosynthesis

Psychosynthesis was developed by the Italian neurologist, psychoanalyst, and psychiatrist Roberto Assagioli during the first half of the twentieth century. He was heavily influenced by Freud and Jung, but disagreed with both of them for a number of reasons. His ideas are far more Jungian than Freudian in that he was keen on promoting a kind of spiritual consciousness. But he thought that Jung didn't grant nearly enough importance to the imagination. He also objected to what he saw as the Freudian tendency to place too much stress on a person's early history. He believed that the future was just as important as the past in terms of how it impacted on the present. Assagioli's idea was that the future existed in the present as the promise of growth and change.

Like Freud and Jung, Assagioli believed that a person's symptom wasn't a pathological manifestation that needed immediate clearing up, but that it came out of a personal crisis that deserved attention. If you took people's symptoms seriously—their depressions, fears, anxieties, and so on—then they would help you to understand the person better. If you could learn what was at stake in the symptom, you could help people find ways to live differently. For someone working in this area, a symptom may be a very *good* sign. If treated sensitively, it might make possible the emergence of a more authentic self. If a psychological "illness" is a person's way of announcing that there's something in their life that they aren't quite coping with, then it may also be a trigger for working out what they really want. Perhaps their writer's block is a protest against their unhappy marriage, or their constant migraines are a sign that they can no longer bear to work for their father's firm. Psychosynthesis would try to help them find ways to follow their real feelings, and achieve a greater sense of wholeness and inner harmony.

The "synthesis" refers to this sense of being at one with oneself and the universe. Therapists of this kind try to take into account a person's emotional, mental, physical, and spiritual wellbeing. So, like the integrative therapists, they believe that a person can reach a state of internal accord. But unlike them, they make no claims to have done any empirical research into the best possible therapeutic methods. This may or may not be a strike in their favour, according to your own ideas about reality. Therapists in this tradition aren't impressed by certainties, moral or otherwise. They would be far more likely to encourage people to bear *un*certainty in the search for their own unique truth. But they may be helped in this direction by an under-lying belief in the idea that the universe is designed to help human consciousness develop. Part of human-kind's tragedy, according to this theory, is due to its separation or alienation from the divine. So healing oneself is seen as something like a spiritual quest.

As well as putting faith in the healing power of the psychotherapeutic relationship, therapists in this field use meditation, visualization, movement, free-form drawing, and writing. They may also encourage their clients to cry, swear, or scream if they need to. Per-haps because people with a training in psychosynthesis have such a strong sense of the goodness of the world and of humans, they feel safe enough to let people try out almost any form of expression. All of it is bound to lead somewhere worthwhile. A therapist of this sort will "listen to the soul" of the client and will tend to see artistic expression as a means of coaxing out its "lost language".

As well as the unconscious and the conscious mind, this group have the notion of a "superconscious". This would be the part of the mind that is engaged in "peak experiences". These would be experiences of the sub-lime, perhaps characterized by a sense of bliss and oneness with the universe. Peak experiences might typically happen in relation to nature, but may just as well take place on a busy high street or in a night-club. They involve an incredible sense of connected-ness, with people, or even with things. (People who take psychotropic drugs also use the term "peaking" to describe a moment of maximum excitement and joy.) While some psychiatrists, and other kinds of therapists, may put experiences like this down to mania or even to the onset of a psychosis, for people trained in psychosynthesis, a "peak experience" would be something more like the sign of a spiritual awakening.

This group aren't alone in seeing these sorts of phenomena as a good thing. In the 1960s, the psychologist Abraham Maslow wrote extensively about these sorts of ecstatic states and concluded that they had great therapeutic value. After an event like this, a person may find themselves with a renewed sense of enthusiasm or creativity. They may find that their relationships are positively affected in the aftermath of a brush with transpersonal unity. Maslow concluded that peak experiences were very good for people and were generally to be encouraged. Unfortunately, the most reliable means of bringing them about is by taking ecstasy, LSD, or magic mushrooms, and not everyone's that way inclined. But if you just happen to have such an experience and are undergoing psychosynthesis, then your therapist will no doubt be very pleased for you.

Psychosynthesis is clearly an exciting option for people with an interest in cosmic balance. It's a very openminded, open-ended approach that really lets people develop in their own idiosyncratic way.

Systemic therapy

This type of therapy is usually associated with families and other kinds of group. It has its roots in systems theory and cybernetics, that is, the study of the ways in which the different components of a system affect one another. If the mention of cybernetics makes it sound a little inhuman, it's perhaps worth mentioning that systems theory has plenty to say about the incredible complexity of interrelation, whether in the fields of mathematics and computer design or in personal relationships. Chaos theory is a branch of systems theory that speaks about the impossibility of making long-term predictions. You can try to say what the weather will be like tomorrow by looking at the weather today and attempting to make calculations by weighing up wind speeds, thermodynamics, and humidity. But very often you will get it wrong because weather systems are too complex to be predicted with any great certainty. Still, you can estimate that a high westerly wind is likely to cause a drop in temperatures, and sometimes you'll be right.

So, systemic psychotherapists look at the complex interactions between members of a group. They believe that by isolating individuals and treating them separately, you risk losing a sense of their place in their surroundings. Given that people's relationships, either at work or at home, are very likely to have a huge impact on their lives (and if they don't, that's a worrying sign in itself), then these should be looked at in the therapy. A family systems therapist would see as many members of a family as would like to come along. They might not all be able to be there for every session, but by turning up they would not only be able to explain their position in the family as they understand it, but might also demonstrate for the therapist something of the dynamics between themselves and other family members. The therapist will be on the lookout for patterns of behaviour and actions that trigger particular reactions. They might spot that one person's quietness makes another person anxious and volatile, or they may see how certain family members go out of their way to placate others.

Still, because systemic people are post-modern and wise to chaos, they won't simply make a quick summary of what's going on and tell you how to do it differently.

Systemic therapists work by giving what they call little "nudges" here and there and seeing how they impact on the overall scheme. If they notice that someone always reacts in a certain way to a particular thing, they may ask whether there might be a possibility of responding differently. Of course, this new type of response will have knock-on effects and these may need to be looked at too. The idea is just that systems alter themselves, and that little changes will affect everything else. A family may even be dealing with the aftermath of a change—a death or marriage that has had a huge impact on the way everyone relates—and the very reordering of the old system may be unsettling in itself. The aim of this sort of therapy isn't to engineer the perfect family, just to help people out of any knots or deadlocks that they may have got themselves into.

A systemic therapist won't tend to be interested in the underlying causes of the problem. They won't be trying to discover each person's deep-seated reasons for behaving in the ways that they do. The focus will be largely on the present. You could argue that this is either a strength or a weakness of the treatment. On the one hand, if you tried to take each group member's own complexity into account, you might never get round to seeing how the whole group functioned. But on the other hand, you might say that by treating each person as a unit in a complex system you are overriding something of their individual systemic intricacy.

Surely they are each struggling with all of the different forces at work in them. In the way that you might find it just as fascinating to study a ten-centimetre cube of air as the entire weather system over Europe, it may be just as worthwhile to look closely at a single person as to investigate a whole society (although that single person will be a product of their society, so the distinction will never be simple).

You can't say that systemic therapy is better because it takes a broader view, but you *can* say it's another valid way of coming at the problem. If a family or group feel inclined to go along and try this sort of thing together, then it may be extremely helpful and worthwhile. The big advantage of family therapy is that the therapist ought to be alert to the fact that one person's behaviour can affect the entire group. Still, if you feel like your family as a whole is the problem, it doesn't necessarily follow that the only way to deal with it is to force them all to go and see a shrink together. Apart from the fact that they may not want to, it's certainly not the only way to change your relation to them. Like the famous butterfly of chaos theory, you might just as well affect the entire system by flapping your own wings your own way.

Brief therapies and life coaching

This section will focus on a variety of quick "cures". Some, like hypnotherapy, are likely to involve trained, accredited practitioners. Others, like life coaching, can be more of an unknown quantity. But, as before, the idea will be to give a broad view of what you might be able to expect from each treatment and not to recommend some and warn against others. As you'll see, some of the principles mentioned in the previous chapter reappear, but in slightly different ways.

Brief therapy

This description could be applied to any form of therapy that takes place in the short term (six to twelve sessions). But it is also used more specifically in titles like solution-focussed brief therapy, or SFBT. It may even describe forms of therapy that aim to be effective in a single session. This last kind of treatment is quite unusual and may involve anything from a client performing a specially designed ritual with a therapist, to undergoing some kind of controlled ordeal, or simply describing how their life would be if their problems miraculously vanished. Some people may even find themselves undergoing therapy of this sort without realizing. I had a friend who was very depressed and hadn't been able to get out of bed for weeks. He telephoned a number of therapists, some of whom offered to treat him by telephone, while others said that they were very sorry, but if he couldn't make it to their consulting room they wouldn't be able to work with him. Eventually, another friend recommended someone, saying he was very eminent and brilliant. The man rang this therapist and was sternly ordered to jump in a taxi and get over there at once. He was so taken aback that he did just that. But when the taxi pulled up outside the therapist's house, he suddenly had the sense that he was better. He'd got out of bed, got dressed, and crossed town. He didn't actually need to *see* the therapist at all. So he leapt out of the taxi, took the Tube home, and promptly pronounced himself cured. This must surely qualify as the briefest therapy ever—it was over before it began—but it had real effects, at least in the short term.

That sort of cure might make six sessions of SFBT seem a bit sluggish. But if you think you can afford the time, SFBT is a form of therapy that promises to focus on solutions rather than problems. Relaxation and visualization may form part of this sort of treatment, alongside discussions that aim to provide actionable solutions to whatever it is you're suffering from. SFBT therapists are interested in the present and the future, and don't give much credence to the past. Like many proponents of brief therapies, they argue that giving too much importance to past events is liable to make the situation worse rather than better.

A typical SFBT approach would be to ask the client to envision a perfect future. The client will then, together with their therapist, take a look at their current situation in order to see which elements of their life support the possibility of this future, and which elements work against it. From here, they can decide what to keep doing and what to stop. As you can see, it's a very pragmatic approach that might work extremely well in some circumstances and totally miss the mark in others. For instance, if a very overweight person turns up with a vision of the future in which they are thin, the most straightforward solution may be to keep eating salad and stop eating cake. But they are sure to know this already, and to have tried extremely hard to do it. Still, the fact that they feel strongly enough to go and see a therapist about it—and perhaps even to pay a substantial fee—may be the very thing that makes it possible to stick to their diet this time. Especially if the therapist is a sympathetic, serious person who makes them feel capable of doing what they say they want to do. On the other hand, the thing that made them over-eat in the first place will remain unaddressed. The fact that these sorts of questions are left unanswered may mean that any change is short-lived. Or it may just happen that the weight loss cheers them up so much that they no longer need to comfort themselves with chocolate.

This is the kind of choice you constantly come up against in therapy. Do you try for quick results at the risk of a superficial fix that doesn't last? Or do you risk wasting time and money on an open-ended treatment with no guarantees? You can find plenty of people who are prepared to defend either option dogmatically, but there can surely be no definitive answer. You just have to use your intuition about the approach that will work best for you.

In case it helps either way, I noticed a funny thing on a website for a Harley Street clinic specializing in brief therapies. It talked about "microwave culture", the terrible bustle and speed of modern life, and offered people an alternative space to come and discuss their difficulties. At the same time, it promised effectiveness within a limited time frame, and a treatment that wouldn't interfere too much with clients' lives. While these offers may be commendable, you can also see how they echo the problem they are aiming to solve. They offer a kind of "microwave therapy". But if you feel that all you need is a bit of a nudge, rather than a major dismantling, then this might be precisely the sort of thing you want to hear. And if you are *really* lucky, you may find yourself cured before you even start anyway.

Emotional brain training (EBT)

This is a "new" approach, developed by Laurel Mellin in America over the last three decades. At least, it claims to be a revolutionary, scientific approach to unhappiness but, in practice, its techniques are rather like a mixture of meditation, prayer, self-hypnosis, and cognitive therapy. The big idea is that you can rewire your brain—and swiftly move from stress to joy—using a few simple exercises. These include the repetition of certain phrases, the questioning of unrealistic expectations, and the really ground-breaking practice of saying what's up. If you follow the instruction manual (or the EBT app on your iPhone), your neural pathways will soon get the message and start functioning in such a way as to make your life much better.

We are invited by Mellin to imagine a future a decade from now in which everyone is naturally joyful. No one needs drugs any more because they have all learned how to rewire themselves like a bunch of good little androids. You might wonder what would happen to the people who chose to resist the joy regime. Would they be punished? Or would their foolish resistance to the good life be punishment enough in itself?

Luckily, it's never going to come to that. I feel I can say this with some confidence because there has been quite a lot of experimentation in this field over the last few millennia. You might equally say that if everyone were a practising Buddhist, or followed Christian doctrine, then the world would be a more peaceful and joyous place. For whatever reason, these life-improving praxes have failed to catch on to the point where wars have become unnecessary and humankind lives harmoniously. They certainly help some people a great deal, but they aren't so infallible that the whole world can get behind them and stroll forward into a stress-free, non-neurotic future.

Naturally, it can be extremely useful to have some strategies ready for when you're feeling terrible, and EBT offers precisely that. It's just that it can't claim that it has anything like a unique answer to the question of human suffering. It sells itself as the latest scientific breakthrough on the grounds that it ties tried-and-tested methods, like self-questioning and speaking, together with new developments in neuroscience. But, in practice, it's nothing new. The only difference between EBT and its predecessors—therapy and religion—is in the conceptual framework it offers. If you repeat certain phrases or try to be calm and kind, does it actually matter whether you are doing it because you think it serves God or because you believe it has an effect on your "wiring"? If the latter is actually the case, then you would surely get the same result even if you were praying or meditating for the former reason. And people have been trying that for quite some time now ...

It may be that, for some people, science offers a better set of motivations for doing things than religion ever did. They would never be able to chant to themselves if they thought they had to believe in God for it to matter. But they are more than happy to chant if it's in the name of retraining their neural networks. So EBT could be said to be an attempt at an updated religion. You get all the good bits, weeded of the embarrassingly unscientific mythologies. Still, apart from the fact that it actually goes down extremely well with certain American Christians—it's a great bit of scientific back-up for whatever they were doing already—it also risks bringing with it the dogma that so often comes with religious belief. The general drift of writing on EBT is that it's perfectly easy to do away with suffering. The implication is therefore that, if you are suffering, it's your fault for not training your brain better. The end result of a belief system like this is a kind of emotional fascism; if the tools are there to fix yourself, then why aren't you using them? Happily, most people aren't that stupid.

Hypnotherapy and hypno-analysis

The most common therapeutic use of hypnosis is as part of a cognitive or behaviourally oriented treatment. Whether you go because you want to give up smoking, or because you are depressed or anxious, you will almost certainly be invited to tell the therapist a bit about your life and your current situation—you won't simply be put into a trance at the beginning of the session. As well as finding out a bit about who you are, the therapist will need to establish whether you are a good candidate for hypnosis. If the very idea terrifies you, or if you are very resistant to suggestion, then it may not work. But an experienced hypnotist will have techniques for working with less straightforward cases. If you're nervous or dubious, they will just have to try a different approach. However, if you are going against your will—because a partner has told you to, for example—then there's less hope of the treatment having any great effect.

Hypnosis involves being put into a sleep-like state. In this state, if all goes well, you will become highly suggestible. This basically means that you will take what your therapist says much more seriously than you would if you were fully awake. If they say that the smell of smoke will become disgusting to you, or that you will feel much happier when you wake up in the mornings, then this may really happen. They might test you to see whether or not you have arrived at this ideal state. For example, they may tell you that your arm has become as light as a feather and that it is floating upwards, away from the arm of the chair. If it actually does, then you are ready to be told how smelly and unwholesome cigarettes are. When you wake up, this idea will hopefully stay with you as if it is an idea of your own.

Some people are far more suggestible than others, and this will have an effect on the success of the therapy. Perhaps more so than any other treatment, hypnotherapy relies on your thinking it's a good idea, and on believing that your therapist is a decent, trustworthy person. Unlike other treatments in which the discussions you have may be very open-ended, leaving it up to you to draw your own conclusions, hypnotherapy really does involve being told what to do. However, the fact that you've already told the other person what you want them to tell you to do means that you are likely to be inclined to agree to do it. Hypnotic techniques can fail, even with a very suggestible person, if the hypnotist tries to get them to do things that they object to or feel are against their best interests. So, in spite of the bad press generated by a few stage hypnotists, it's generally a safe treatment.

One of the strangest things about hypnosis is how un-strange it is. Being hypnotized in a therapeutic context just feels like being more relaxed and comfortable than usual, as opposed to being in a weird, altered state. You will often be able to remember everything that's happened to you, including everything that's been said.

Hypno-analysis is a very different branch of hypnotherapy that involves encouraging people to dredge up lost memories. As opposed to using the suggestible state to get people to give up unwanted behaviours— or to adopt more desirable ones—hypno-analysts hope to unlock parts of the psyche that have previously been inaccessible.

This technique has quite a venerable history, but has recently fallen into disrepute. It was used by Breuer and Freud in the earliest days of psychoanalysis. They had the idea that by speaking about repressed traumatic memories while under hypnosis, the patient would experience a kind of catharsis which would result in the reduction of neurotic symptoms. Hypnosis was used to bypass the inhibitions that may have prevented patients from speaking about difficult and/or sexually explicit material. Freud stopped using it partly because he believed that things said under hypnosis seemed to have a different currency to things said while awake. He decided that everything uttered in analysis should be said in a normal waking state, otherwise it was too easy to write it off as being somehow separate from life.

Hypnosis was also used with shell-shocked soldiers during both world wars, to help them deal with traumatic events. But during the 1990s, there were court cases, mainly in America, in which therapists were accused of producing false memory syndrome in patients. If a therapist decided that a patient's symptoms were due to an experience of abuse, which the patient had since managed to forget, then they might use hypnosis in order to make the "memory" accessible again. The problem is that, because people are so suggestible in that state, they may produce a "memory" of something that never actually happened. If they get the sense that their therapist is certain they were abused, then they might respond to this implicit suggestion by producing a scene or an event that would satisfy the therapist.

In the mid-1990s, after working on a court case detailing how false memory syndrome following a hypnosis had led a daughter to convict her father of a murder he didn't commit, the American professor Elizabeth

Loftus devised an experiment to see how easy it was to produce a false memory. Subjects were told that their families had provided a list of memories of fairly insignificant things from their past. They were then presented with an outline of each event and asked to add any details they could recall. But mixed in with all the real events was a fictional one; they were told that they'd got lost in a shopping mall some time between the ages of four and six. Out of twenty-four participants, five "remembered" being lost in the mall and added details.

If you're interested in hypnotherapy, it's important to know which type of therapist you're talking to. The first kind of therapy—the more behaviourally oriented—is extremely popular and widely practised, while the second is perhaps slightly less common. If you like the sound of hypno-analysis but find the idea of false memory syndrome rather terrifying, it's as well to remember that those cases are extremely rare. Still, it would certainly be wise to discuss any fears you might have about this with the therapist and to have some sense of the kind of person you're dealing with before you let yourself be hypnotized.

Aside from these two uses of hypnosis, there's also past-life regression therapy, which is something more like palmistry or fortune-telling, that is, not within the remit of this book (although it's obviously very uplifting for some people to "discover" that they used to be Catherine the Great).

Life coaching

This category has so many subcategories that it's hard to even think about giving it an overall definition. As well as life coaching *per se*, there's dating coaching, relationship coaching, business coaching, health coaching, parent coaching, and organizational coaching, amongst other types. There's nothing in the term "coaching" that tells you about the practitioner's background. They may be anything from a very experienced psychotherapist to a self-designated helpful person. They may also be a psychologist with no formal clinical training. Or even a psychiatrist or psychoanalyst from abroad whose professional title doesn't carry over to their new country. Because "life coach" is an unregulated term, anyone can use it. There are courses in life coaching, but they are also very variable. Some trainings might lead to a recognized qualification, while others don't. At worst, coaching trainings themselves are money-making schemes that promise all sorts of rewards but deliver very little.

Life coaching could take numerous forms. It's not unusual for people to offer to do it over the phone, or even on Skype. A life coach might just as well come to your house as expect you to go and see them. The work might involve anything from conversation, to list-writing and homework, to having someone look through your cupboards and tell you what to throw away and what to keep. The most popular types of life coaching would take a common-sense approach to self-improvement; if you want things to be different, you take steps to change them—it's that simple. Life coaching often has a lot in common with cognitive and behavioural treatments, but it's even less inclined to bother itself with the past or with the unconscious. The most likely approach would be to treat the problem in the present in the most practical way possible. If you never get a date, you may be instructed to join an agency, try speed dating, or go off on murder mystery weekends. You may also be told how to dress, and even how to conduct a conversation: "Show an interest in the other person. Don't put yourself down. Don't mention how much you hate your exes." But, as with sports coaching, the practical advice may be accompanied by all sorts of motivational and encouraging talk: "You must do it because if you don't do it, no one's going to do it for you. But you can do it, you're great, you have the power to change your own destiny, etc." The subtlety of both the solutions and the persuasions will depend on the character and intelligence of the practitioner. Some people are incredibly good at affecting others. It's a strange skill and may exist in some people to an unusual degree. A football manager can earn millions if it seems he can make a drastic difference to his team's performance. A life coach too may very well be able to get you to do all sorts of things you've been unable to do under your own steam. And of course, this would be partly to do with their charisma, and partly to do with the fact that you want those things enough in the first place to hire a life coach to help you achieve them.

One thing to watch out for with life coaching is the likelihood that the person will be equipped only to push you, not to understand you. They are not normally the people to go to to deal with deep-seated psychological problems. This can sometimes be a difficult distinction to call. You might think you just need to clean your cupboards, but your spouse might think you need to deal with your mutually destructive relationship with your mother. This can only be a matter of opinion—and both of you may have a point.

Neurolinguistic programming

Neurolinguistic programming, or NLP, was developed in the 1970s by a psychologist called Richard Bandler and a linguist called John Grinder. They were interested in the effects of language on neurological processes, and the ways in which people may be able to "programme" their emotional and behavioural responses using certain patterns of speech. It has a lot in common with behaviourally oriented hypnotherapy in that the aim is to bring about change by using suggestion. It is entirely result-driven—the whole point is to produce tangible effects as fast as possible. Huge claims have been made on behalf of NLP in this area—it is often presented as a kind of magic cure.

In fact, NLP is so magical that some of its techniques are actually adopted by magicians, who use it to cause people to pick out certain cards from a pack or to temporarily adopt odd beliefs or behaviours. Unlike traditional hypnosis, NLP persuasion techniques can be applied without the subject (or the audience, if there is one) being aware of what's going on. By stressing particular words or fragments of sentences, and by using body language in certain ways, an experienced NLP practitioner/magician should be able to make you do or think things as if of your own free will. For example, they may show you a set of six objects and ask you to pick one. They will tell you that they have predicted in advance which one you'll choose. While you are deciding, they will talk to you about the objects, and perhaps touch them or point at them, in such a way as to make you choose the object of *their* choice, not yours. You will, ideally, have no idea that they are doing this. You will just think they are being chatty and nice. These techniques are very successful, at least with suggestible people.

Another "magical" aspect of NLP has to do with its theories about reading the responses of other people. There's the idea that you can tell a lot about how a person thinks by studying their eye movements. If they look up a lot while they are speaking then they are thinking in visual mode, while sideways eye movements indicate auditory thinking (a focus on sound), and downward glances suggest kinaesthetic thinking (which privileges feeling and sensation). There is some question as to whether any of this is actually true but, depending on who you ask, there is a possibility that there may be something in it. Still, it's far from hard science—and the problems really start when teachers, who've done a workshop or two in NLP, begin "diagnosing" their pupils as "visuals", "verbals", or "kinaesthetics" and treating them accordingly. One common outcome of this, in the case of small children, is that the naughty, jumpy ones are all diagnosed as kinaesthetics and given little silicone toys to fidget with in class. This not only marks them out from the others, but often makes the others jealous—why are the naughty ones given toys?

Another common use is in the field of business, where NLP-informed eye readings might dictate how you communicate with the person you want to manipulate. If you think they are a visual thinker, you use images to persuade them, while auditory thinkers may like speech and music, and kinaesthetics might submit to your will if you present your case using tactile handouts—and maybe you can doubly endear yourself by touching them from time to time.

The arguments against NLP certainly aren't that it isn't clever—it clearly is—but that, in its therapeutic capacity, it may not help people as much as it claims to. In other words, it's quite magical, but is it actually a cure? While the techniques may be ingenious, some people believe that they may be more appropriate to advertisers and pick-up artists than to people with complex personal problems. Neal Strauss's book *The Game* describes his use of NLP "patterns" on unsuspecting women. Apparently, it gave him a great advantage when it came to getting lots of casual sex—he could make people think it was a good idea to sleep with him—but it certainly didn't help him to understand the women afterwards. And it surely didn't help the women, not that this was his aim. The point was quite explicitly to extract enjoyment from them without them kicking up too much fuss.

NLP is genuinely spectacular when it comes to getting people to do things, but it doesn't necessarily offer a space to explore difficult ideas or feelings. And it certainly doesn't promote fair and considerate relations between humans. Perhaps one of the things that's stopped NLP becoming popular as a therapeutic treatment is the fact that it produces very imbalanced power relations. It potentially gives one person far too much power over another (which may be why the army don't object to using it). And, unlike in traditional hypnosis, there's no need for the power to be handed over consensually—NLP patterns can be used on you without you even knowing it's happening. So while an individual NLP therapist might be the sweetest and most well-meaning person on the planet, they are working within a paradigm that's totally antithetical to many therapists' ideas about ethical relations.

As with all treatments that aim only to address surface phenomena rather than underlying causes, there's the question of what happens to a person when their symptom is suddenly snatched away. Defenders of brief therapies say that the removal of the symptom generally has a positive effect on a person's self-esteem, and that deep change is often brought about as a result of this. Attackers say that the unaddressed psychological material just manifests itself in a different way, and that "self-esteem" is a bogus notion anyway—the point in therapy isn't to make people believe they're great, it's to help them inhabit the world without excessive suffering. In fact, high self-esteem may sometimes be quite delusional—one of the false beliefs that a person might be better off giving up. You occasionally hear about people who have become so unbearable as a result of therapy that their friends all want to run a mile. Whereas before they were endearingly self-doubting, now they know exactly where their boundaries are and won't take any nonsense from anyone. This may be because either they or their therapist have fed their fantasies of omnipotence under the guise of "improving self-esteem". Again, this type of "cure" may be short-lived. It's hard to feel brilliant when no one likes you.

Psychoanalysis

Depending on your point of view, psychoanalysis might be the most deep-reaching and serious of all the talking therapies, or it could be a discredited theory, and a terrible waste of time and money. Alternatively, it might seem like a bit of a mystery. What would mark it out from all the other kinds of treatment? Is it really any different? And, if so, how? Is it the only one you do lying on a couch? Do you have to do it five days a week? And will it necessarily culminate in the discovery that you're secretly in love with one of your parents?

The question of what makes a talking cure a psychoanalysis is hotly contested. For some people, it has to be conducted by someone trained under the auspices of the IPA (International Psychoanalytical Association). Anyone else calling themselves a psychoanalyst is a charlatan, apparently. For other people, it would depend on the length of time in treatment and the number of sessions a week (anything less than three days a week and it's psychotherapy). But then again, it can be argued that the psychoanalyticness (or not) of the work can't be measured in terms of institutional sanctions, nor the number of hours clocked up on the couch; it has much more to do with the analytic capacity of the patient. You can get someone to lie down and talk endlessly about dreams to the most eminent of orthodox shrinks and they still won't take their own unconscious into any serious consideration—even if they have an MA in Freudian theory and claim to want to be a psychoanalyst themselves. While the external conditions of psychoanalysis are being met, no actual psychoanalytic work takes place. As a counterpoint to this, you might find someone with no experience in the field who turns up to see a counsellor at their GP's office. They are attentive to every slip of their tongue and are brilliant at following unlikely trains of thought, leading to uncomfortable realizations. They also free-associate, show a natural flair for interpreting dreams, and are sensitive to the dynamics of the transference. If you wanted, you could argue that this person is more engaged in psychoanalytic work than their more psychoanalytically enamoured counterpart. According to this definition, psychoanalysis is something more like the practice of trying to access the unconscious. Freud did it all by himself—what with there being no other psychoanalysts around yet.

In the way that art school can't make you an artist, seeing a psychoanalyst can't make you be psychoanalysed. It's something you can only really engage with yourself—although, like art-making, it can help greatly not to do it in a vacuum.

Already that gives you a pretty weird and skewed view of what psychoanalysis might be. Not to mention the fact that this definition relies on the notion of the unconscious, which is already quite an obscure concept. It gets bandied about a lot, but what exactly is it? Other treatments, like cognitive analytic therapy and hypnotherapy, also claim to have something to say about unconscious thought processes. They both agree that your symptoms, or the things that make you unhappy, are informed by ideas or thoughts that you may have blocked out. If you don't know why you do what you do or feel what you feel, then this must surely be the case. But then there's the question of how you access the stuff that's gone AWOL. Are there theories that can tell you where and how to look for it? Can a trained professional see straight away all the things that you can't?

There is an episode of *Friends* where one of the characters (Phoebe) starts dating a psychoanalyst. He upsets and offends everyone by telling them immediately what's going on with them—they are needy and attention-seeking thanks to the fact that their parents divorced when they were three, say. He gets it right every time, but it doesn't win him any points because nobody wants to hear it. It's funny and excruciating for shrinks to watch because this is exactly what we're supposedly trained *not* to do. Not only does psychoanalytic theory *not* give you the tools to diagnose people on the spot, but it warns against making wild interpretations.

When a shorter treatment claims to be able to have an effect on the unconscious, it is talking about something quite different to the kinds of unconscious effects you might be looking at in psychoanalysis. For instance, in hypnotherapy there's the idea that the therapist can access a deeper layer of your psyche while you are under hypnosis. If they tell you that you will no longer suffer from angry outbursts, then maybe you really won't. But you may never know what the unconscious cause of those outbursts was. It's just that, for whatever reason, the deeper layer of your psyche has accepted the authority of the therapist. In CAT, there's more of an idea that the underlying causes of things need to be articulated in order for change to take place. But if there's no simple key to what makes people do the things they do (phobia = excessive love for parent; eating disorder = excessive hate, etc.), then it will necessarily take time to find out what each individual person has constructed their symptom out of. Still, at the beginning of any treatment, you may have a hunch that a person's rather saccharine account of their lovely, brilliant brother, say, masks a host of darker feelings. In shorter treatments, hunches like this will have to be followed up faster, and may come to form the core of the discussions. A map of the most obvious cracks in the person's story becomes the skeleton of the treatment—so you can hate your lovely brother a bit more, stop feeling so sorry for your Mum, and admit to yourself that you compete with your father. And thus you will also be able to feel better about your male colleagues, less afraid of your girlfriend's moods, and stop getting into squabbles with your boss. You're cured.

In psychoanalysis, these sorts of ideas may also be very important, and an exploration of them may lead to quite similar outcomes. Or you may go a little further and say that your hatred of your brother masks an erotic attraction to him. Or that the pity you feel for your Mum blots out the terrifying sense that she is somehow all-powerful. One of the big differences between analysis and shorter treatments is that, not only do you have time to look beyond first hunches, but you follow through the aftermath of these sorts of discoveries *in* the treatment, rather than being given a course of action at the end. One serious advantage of this is that you can then go on to look at the effects of any changes you are making in your life, and to discuss the consequences of them with your analyst.

For example, if someone comes into treatment because of an unusual sexual preference, they may be faced with a choice between giving it up or trying to live with it. They might initially prefer the first option and will try to understand how they came to like that particular thing so much, in the hope that they will be able to analyse it out of existence. They attempt to uncover the unconscious reasoning that led them to long for that particular activity. If that doesn't work—they now know something about *why* they like it, but it doesn't seem to have put them off—they may then start to look into the second option. They will try to live with it—but how? Will they pay prostitutes to do it with them? And will they try to have "normal" relationships at the same time? Will they join a community of people who also like the same thing? What if this reinforces their idea that their sexuality makes them a social outcast? Or what if there's no one in that select group whom they fancy? Will they then try to incorporate certain aspects of their fetish into relationships with people they actually like? And what will these people feel about it? This sort of process may take years, and it may be incredibly frustrating and disappointing along the way. But it can be very helpful to do it in dialogue with someone who can listen and not dictate, and who knows something about why you may have developed this preference in the first place—and who doesn't hold it against you. You may not end up with a perfectly neat solution, but you will be far wiser about the kinds of enjoyment you can hope to get out of life.

Which brings us to the aim of psychoanalysis. Rather than providing quick relief, psychoanalysis can give you a place to look into all aspects of being human, and to offer you a chance to invent unique solutions to the problems of your own existence. While other treatments might undertake to remove symptoms within a limited time frame, psychoanalysis promises nothing of the sort. It's possible that, during an analysis, you might shake off a phobia, become less anxious, or begin a long-term relationship for the first time in your life. But you might also find it helps you to live *with* your symptom. Perhaps you see how your obsessive rituals help you to organize the world around you. Or you understand that your erratic love life makes it possible for you to write movie scripts. Or maybe even that your crazed clothes shopping is a creative outlet, and that it has probably saved you from self-harming or becoming fatally anorexic.

Still, if you are afraid of flying and your boss is insisting you take a plane to a meeting next week, psychoanalysis might not seem the obvious option. But while a treatment like hypnotherapy *may* achieve results quicker, it might also never cause you to investigate your relationship with your autocratic boss—and in this way, by "curing" you, it could simply allow you to keep an undesirable situation afloat for longer.

Having spoken about psychoanalysis like it's all one thing, it'll be necessary to break the section down into different schools. In keeping with the entire psychotherapeutic field, psychoanalysis is split into warring factions. There are the Jungians, the Kleinians, the Lacanians, and the relational psychoanalysts, all of whom have very different ideas of how to go about things. Not to mention the Freudians—although they are a funny group because any of the others might also claim to be a member. Lacanians in particular might even consider themselves *more* Freudian than the average Freudian, thanks to Lacan's insistence on the careful re-reading of Freud.

Each group has its own ideas about everything from the length of sessions to the importance of infantile sexuality to the best way of responding to the transference. Different groups fare differently in various parts of the world. Klein and the British post-Freudians have top billing in the UK, but are perhaps seen as less important elsewhere. Lacanian psychoanalysis—which is viewed with great suspicion in Britain—is the commonest form of analysis all over Europe and Latin America, particularly in Argentina, one of the most psychoanalysed populations on the planet. Jung is apparently popular in Japan, where his ideas echo traditional ideas about dream interpretation and archetypes. Relational psychoanalysis is the newest development. It originated in the USA and the UK in the 1990s, but is gaining ground in the rest of Europe. And, of course, Freud is admired and reviled everywhere.

Freudian psychoanalysis

All psychoanalysis is, loosely speaking, Freudian. But what does that actually mean? Freud had some pretty strange ideas about women—so do these still persist in contemporary analysis, or has it been updated? And is Freudian analysis the one where the analyst simply sits there in silence—in which case, who cares what they think about women, or any other subject, if they're never going to say anything anyway?

To answer the second question first, all Freudian analysts will be bound to have quite different styles, depending on the kind of person they are, and the kind of person they were analysed by. Some are very quiet, and some are almost garrulous (at least by shrinky standards). This has been true since the very beginnings of the profession. Freud wrote very little about technique, and his immediate circle all seem to have developed quite different ways of working, just like any other group of doctors. Freud himself certainly spoke in sessions, asked questions, made interpretations, and explained the basic principles of psychoanalysis. The idea of an analyst as a totally blank screen is something that came later. So a Freudian analyst will be as personable or as inscrutable as they see fit.

In terms of updating Freud's theories, he had so many different ideas at different times that you'd be incredibly unlikely to find a Freudian who's stuck to the letter of Freud's work—because sticking to one letter might involve the refutation of another. In terms of his ideas about gender, it's true that he came out with some pretty strange-sounding notions about women. That they try to get over not having penises by having babies. That they can't be threatened with castration so they are less law-abiding. And that, naturally, a young girl would want to have an affair with her father's friend, given that she can't have her father (as in the famously hideous Dora case). Still, in spite of trying out lots of different theoretical possibilities, he maintained that he didn't understand women very well. The advantage of this was that he made it his mission to listen to them and to try to understand them better. So any Freudian worth his or her salt will do the same. It's also worth remembering that Freud had lots of brilliant female friends and colleagues, that he didn't frown on women's sexual desires, that he thought both men and women should be granted more sexual freedom, and that he didn't think homosexuality was an illness. In other words, he was extremely open-minded and keen on letting people be. This, one hopes, is still the case with Freudian analysts. Or at least it ought to be rare to come across one who is stuck with Victorian ideas about gender.

Another commonly held view about Freudian analysis is that everything in your life will be reduced to sex. This, of course, is grossly unfair. People who say this are obviously forgetting the importance of violence. Yes, it's true, in Freudian theory, sex and violence feature heavily. Human nature is seen as something rather dark, and anyone who thinks otherwise may be suspected of self-delusion. So the general drift of an analysis of this sort won't be to make you feel like everything's OK. Quite the opposite. It will aim to help you deal with the fact that your intentions may not be entirely honourable at all times, and neither will those of the people around you.

Growing up and becoming civilized is bound to involve a reigning in of your erotic and aggressive impulses. Children may be inclined to cling to the people they love and lash out at the people who threaten to disrupt their selfishness. And they may do both to the same person. They soon work out that this isn't on. As you learn to be more adult about your feelings, you may actually want to believe that you really *are* good. You really *do* love your baby sister, you *want* to tidy your bedroom, you think your father has a point when he tells you off, your own genitals really are off-limits. But almost everything "good" about you is hard won. You're congratulated for doing what doesn't come naturally. You wait for your dinner, you leave the toilet clean, you let other people play with your toys. You're a delight.

If, later, you get depressed or anxious, you do things against your best interests or generally make a mess of your life, perhaps it has something to do with the fact that you've given up too much. You're trying to live by the rules that have been laid out before you, but something about it isn't working. (And, depending on your family, these rules could be anything. Some parents like cheeky children. Maybe you were always congratulated for being able to answer back. And maybe you've just lost your job because of it.) By trying to make yourself loveable, you've made yourself impossible. Or perhaps it's the opposite. You can't give *anything* up. You don't see why you should compromise for the sake of other people. You chase after every satisfaction but end up feeling empty and depleted.

In a long-term Freudian analysis, you should be able to look into every aspect of your history. Anything and everything is fair game, from birth to potty training to first love. Every single significant person in your life might make an appearance. Any story you tell yourself about who you are is available to be put in question. All your defences may be scrutinized. Perhaps your much commented-on kindness grew out of the hatred and envy you felt towards your half-brother. Perhaps your left-wing politics are a way of stating publicly that you *love* to share, the very thing you find it hardest to do in close relationships. Perhaps your fear of being attacked in the night masks a shameful sexual phantasy. Whatever you've made yourself into—in collaboration with the world around you—can be studied bit by bit and reordered or left alone accordingly.

The role of the analyst in all of this is to be both challenging and supportive—two qualities which can sometimes seem mutually exclusive. For Freud, the analytic relation (when it went well) echoed an early relation with a loved person—maybe a parent. The care that your analyst showed you, by listening and not judging, would, with luck, make it possible for you to bear the difficulty of facing yourself in all your dreadful faultiness.

Still, the ultimate goal of Freudian analysis is in dispute, even amongst Freudians. In his earliest writings, Freud suggested that relief necessarily came from the lifting of repression. As soon as you owned up to your underlying ideas and wishes, you felt better. He soon realized that this wasn't actually the case. A symptom might very well persist, in spite of its hidden logic being exposed. So he developed the ideas of remembering, repeating, and working through (which together make up the title of one of his essays). During the analysis, you dredge up memories, and you also repeat earlier relationships or scenarios—either with your analyst or in the rest of your life. Perhaps you have a period of being angry with your analyst because they are useless and can't help you (just like your father). But because you are in treatment, it shouldn't be a simple repetition—you can work something through, scrutinize it, see what you bring to it, and, with luck, understand it differently this time. You can also bring out different facets with each repetition. Having seen how you treat your analyst, you might later notice what you are doing to a particular friend, which will, in turn, tell you something about the way you treat your husband. So this would be one version of a Freudian "cure". Not only do you understand what you are doing on a conceptual level, but you experience yourself doing the sorts of things you do and thereby open up the possibility of doing them differently next time.

However, in the early 1920s, Freud wrote an essay called "The Ego and the Id". In it, he suggested that the point of the ego was largely to mediate between the id and the super-ego. The id represented the drives, and all the erotic, pushy violence that needs to be kept in check, and the super-ego was the bossy agency in charge of doing this. Stuck between the rowdy mob and the police force was the poor old ego—the person's sense of self—trying to cope with the two warring factions. Illness was a result of the ego not being able to do its job properly. Either it was flooded by impulses that it was unable to contain, or it was kept in a stranglehold by a hyper-vigilant conscience. So some post-Freudians proposed that the task of psychoanalysis could be to strengthen up the ego in order to fulfil its function better. This idea is seen by some to be in radical opposition to Freud's earlier proposition that you have to be realistic about who or what you are, and certainly not kid yourself about being rational and in charge. But, for others, it's a very good and practical solution—with a nice, strong ego you won't take any nonsense from anyone. Particularly not yourself. This later idea of Freud's became particularly popular with certain American psychoanalysts, leading to the school of thought known as "ego psychology". (And possibly also leading to those famous L'Oreal adverts.)

So the general aim of Freudian analysis is split off into two very different directions. On the one hand, you may be encouraged to be realistic about the fragmentary and impossible nature of being, and on the other hand, you might be helped to build better armour against internal and external attack. It's an ethical choice, and the path you choose may ultimately be as much up to you as it is up to your analyst. It may even prove possible to elegantly combine the two.

This division is constitutive of the entire field. As you can see from the descriptions of the many therapies above, it now defines the practice of therapy, with different treatments betting on one approach or the other, to varying extremes.

Jungian analysis

Although this one probably shouldn't be in this chapter, it is. Jung himself coined the term "analytical psychology" to describe his theory and practice, and to differentiate it from psychoanalysis. Jungian analysis is very different to psychoanalysis thanks to Jung's unique way of theorizing the unconscious. Instead of being a despository for unacceptable thoughts and feelings, Jung's conception sees it more as a source of healing energy.

Jung not only divides the psyche into conscious and unconscious, but the unconscious itself is split into "personal" and "collective" components. Jung's "personal unconscious" is basically a softer version of the Freudian unconscious. It contains an individual's repressed and forgotten thoughts and memories. This, however, isn't at all the most potent part of the psyche, it's more like a surface distraction. Far more important is the underlying "collective unconscious", which has been formed throughout the evolution of humankind. Rather than an unconscious built out of your own experiences, this one's been honed by thousands of years of human existence.

This process, according to Jung, has culminated in a number of "archetypes" that shape our minds and have huge importance for all humans, irrespective of their cultural background. For example, there's the mother archetype. Everyone on earth has had a mother, whether she was there to bring them up or not. Even the people without biological mothers have been brought up by *someone*. So, says Jung, there has developed in the human psyche a sort of mother-place, an inbuilt capacity for relating to a mother figure. And if your mother/mother replacement was too divergent from the mother archetype, then this will have consequences for you. Likewise with the father archetype. (And a whole load of others, including the child, the trickster, the devil, and the scarecrow.) As you can see, it's not altogether different from the general idea that if you have a dodgy Mum and Dad, it may very well mess you up. But it's a totally distinct way of coming at it. In the first case, it's supposedly all to do with your own unique experiences, while in the second, it's to do with your relation to humankind's unconscious heritage.

Another important Jungian concept is the shadow. The shadow is also an archetype. It's made up of all the parts of a person that they don't want to acknowledge. In attempting to push these things away, it's as if an external entity is created that nonetheless remains very much attached. The disowned qualities are liable to be perceived as residing in other people—you think *they're* mean or jealous when really it's *you*. The more people push away the less savoury aspects of themselves, the darker and more menacing their shadow becomes. A Jungian would encourage you to become more intimate with the shadier side of your character. This would ostensibly enable you to stay in touch with reality a bit better, and may also allow you to be more productive. While the shadow is potentially a destructive force, it's also the seat of creativity; being in touch with your dark side will stop you being a dried-up old stick.

The general aim in Jungian analysis is to bring a person's conscious and unconscious into more harmonious relation. (This process was given the name "individuation".) Again, while this may sound like the aim of Freudian psychoanalysis, it's not at all the same.

Freud didn't set much store by the idea that a person could achieve a state of wholeness or unity—you just had to accept the fact that your unconscious was liable to mess you around and to try to be as wise to its ways as possible.

Not only is the aim different, the kinds of interpretation you'd see along the way would also be poles apart. A Jungian analysis would involve the patient developing some kind of understanding of the codes of the collective unconscious. So a Jungian would look out for evidence of archetypes in the dreams, fantasies, and everyday lives of their patients and help them to see how they may be impacting on their lives. This is very much in opposition to the Freudian idea that people construct their own symbols, and that what means one thing to one person will mean something quite different to another.

One of the most famous uses of Jungian theory is in George Lucas's *Star Wars*. Lucas set out to write a story with very broad appeal and became interested in archetypes and the ways in which certain types of character appeared in traditional stories from all over the world. If these figures were really so deep-rooted in the human psyche, then a film in which they all appeared would surely pull in crowds. Lucas's bet paid off—the whole world loves those movies. (And, to use Luke Skywalker as an example, you can see that if he turned up to see a Jungian analyst, he might be alerted to the fact that Obi Wan Kenobi perfectly embodies the archetype of the "wise old man", Princess Leia is clearly a "maiden", and Darth Vader is a pretty shadowy fellow, who turns out to be far closer to Luke than he might have imagined.)

The idea of a collective unconscious may seem more poetic than scientific, but for many people that is its strength. Jung himself seems to have been far more interested in artistic "truth" than in provable facts. His theories are informed by ideas that resonate throughout human culture. So, while they might be impossible to put to the test, you can't really say he's just being silly.

One of the very serious ways in which Jungian analysis is at odds with other analytic theories is in its comfortable acquiescence to religion and, by extension, all of humankind's myths. For Freud, religion was a fiction that people used to blind themselves to painful realities (and/or to gain control over others). It's a very important part of psychoanalytic theory to come up with answers as to why people are so enthralled by religion and religious stories, or by fictions in general. For most psychoanalytic thinkers, it isn't enough to say that they've always been around so they must be very important. The thing would be to ask how they got there, why people get so stuck on them, and what social and personal functions they serve. To simply say that they are a part of who we are so we ought to get in tune with them might seem a little too blindly accepting. Jung is perhaps a bit like a certain fairy-tale character himself. After Sleeping Beauty has been struck by the evil fairy, a good fairy appears and says, "I can't undo the spell, but I can soften it. Now, instead of dying, the princess will just fall asleep for a hundred years." Likewise, after Freud comes along and says human beings are full of foul impulses and it's amazing that "civilization" has got this far, Jung says it's not that bad, really, and people just need to get in touch with a higher order and everything will be OK.

Still, even Jung himself didn't practise along purely "Jungian" lines. He would mix in elements of Freudian analysis and Adlerian psychology (Alfred Adler being another post-Freudian, who fell out with Freud over the matter of the influence of the social on the individual). Any contemporary Jungian would also be likely to draw from a much broader pool of ideas than just those contained in Jung's work.

Kleinian psychoanalysis and object relations theory

Melanie Klein was a charismatic psychoanalyst who settled in London in the 1920s. Her own analysis wasn't with Freud but with Sandor Ferenczi and then Karl Abraham, two of Freud's close associates. Much is made of the fact that, by keeping a slight distance from Freud, she was able to develop her own unique take on psychoanalysis. Her early work was with children. She would interpret their games in uncompromisingly psychoanalytic terms; she might tell a child that the banging together of certain toys symbolized the banging together of Mummy and Daddy to make a baby. She observed that her forthright statements often had dramatic effects on the children—they would apparently become less anxious and more able to play and communicate.

From working with children, she went on to analyse adults, bringing with her all the ideas she'd developed with her very young analysands. Like Jung, she had the idea that you could access deeper layers of the unconscious than even Freud had talked about. But unlike Jung, she saw the concealed part of the psyche as a bit of a bloodbath—there was nothing "nice" about it whatsoever. If Jung tried to make psychoanalysis a bit sweeter, Klein pushed hard in the opposite direction.

In Klein's universe, babies were full of vicious, hateful impulses towards their carers. (The child, the carers, and their body parts are "objects", and "relations" with them can sometimes be fraught.) The poor infants, in trying to deal with the overwhelming sensations in their bodies, might imagine these were caused by—or at least linked with—the people who fed them, washed them, and put them to bed. These difficult feelings might then be projected outwards into the people around them, thereby making the world a very frightening place. A baby's mother and/or father might be perceived as evil entities. Or alternatively, the baby might experience *itself* as something awful that was putting its lovely parents at risk.

The baby's bizarre perception of the world would lay the ground for interpersonal distortions in later life. Symptoms could be formed out of these confusions between inside and outside. Projecting everything bad onto other people and imagining oneself lily white would lead to a narcissistic character, prone to a delusional sense of persecution, whereas keeping all the bad things inside oneself and seeing other people as perfect could lead to extreme melancholia. In between these two very black and white examples was a plethora of other possibilities resulting in anxiety, depression, obsessional symptoms, phobias, and so on.

In Kleinian analysis, you might be helped to sort your way through the good things and the bad things and to try to develop a better conception of the problems that come from inside and the ones that come from outside. You would, in theory, grow to understand something about what your symptom is made out of. Unlike therapies that give you tougher methods for dealing with bad feelings and for keeping your repressions intact (such as "relaxation techniques" and other distractions), a Kleinian analysis would help you work through the tangles in your psychic structure and study your individual subjective make-up. And one of the most useful tools for doing this, according to Klein and her followers, is the transference. The relationship between the analyst and the patient will provide all sorts of vital clues as to what the patient wants and expects from other people. This leads on to the most noticeable feature of this sort of analysis—what's known as "interpreting the transference". While other schools of analysis and therapy may be very attentive to the patient/practitioner dynamic, object relations people are trained to tackle it head on. If you are late, they may tell you that you are showing your analyst that you are capable of withholding something from them. If you get angry about something during the session, they might ask whether you are angry with them. If you feel miserable on a Friday, they might suggest it's because you won't be seeing them for a few days and are feeling abandoned. Dreams will often be interpreted in terms of whatever's going on in the analysis at the time. It can be quite disconcerting if you aren't expecting it.

The first therapist I saw obviously had a British object relations background, although I didn't know it at the time. I was twenty-three and I don't think he was all that much older. I thought the fact that he was always trying to find out what I felt about him was slightly suspect. Why did he want to know? But then when I went to see a (much older) Lacanian a few years later, I slightly missed the confrontational aspect of the therapy and found my new analyst incredibly opaque and absent. It's not hard to see how bringing the analytic relation to the forefront and really examining it allows a person to experience something in the present, and stops the analysis becoming detached and academic. But there is also sometimes the risk that the analyst may interpret things a bit dogmatically and miss other important unconscious material because they are so focussed on what's happening in the room. One slightly comical example of this comes from a friend of a friend who admired the flowers in her shrink's garden only to be given the immediate response, "Perhaps *you'd* like to be a flower growing in my garden". While, in the right hands, transference interpretations can be very eye-opening, in the wrong hands they can encourage emotionally needy practitioners to over-estimate their importance in their patients' lives.

In the 1950s, Melanie Klein became concerned by the way in which some of her followers were taking up her ideas around transference and counter-transference. Some people had the idea that the feelings the patient projected onto the analyst could actually be felt by the analyst. Instead of saying "projected onto", people began to say "projected *into*", with the implication that the patient's feelings actually arrived intact via a process of emotional osmosis. So, if you felt angry with your patient, it was because the patient had put the anger there, not because you were feeling it due to your own internal conflicts—and needed to deal with it and keep it out of the treatment. In other words, it made the patient responsible for the analyst's feelings during sessions. This meant that a badly analysed practitioner would be able to blame their patient for whatever uncomfortable feelings of love and hate they might experience towards them. So, a good, tactful Kleinian will be very good at spotting things at play in the analytic relation and bringing them out into the open. But a bad, tactless post-Kleinian might force interpretations onto the patient when they ought to be asking themselves some serious questions about their own state of mind.

Kleinian analysis is great for people who really want to understand something about the human condition and their own place in the world, and who aren't too worried about getting rid of their symptoms in a rush. Typically, *all* psychoanalysts tend to see a lot of artists, actors, and writers—and anyone else who has a particular interest in knowing what goes on underneath the surface—whereas people who simply want to be fixed may be more inclined to gravitate towards treatments like CBT, or psychiatric medicine.

Lacanian psychoanalysis

There is the well-known Lacanian answerphone joke: "Please articulate your demand after the beep in order for me not to respond to it." If your idea of a good therapist is someone who can make you feel happy and whole, then this lot may look a bit frightening. Far from wanting to mend you so you can get back into the production line, they are more inclined to let you be as weird as you seem inclined to be. They are also very attuned to the possibility that what you *say* you want isn't what you *actually* want—or at least that human beings are perfectly capable of wanting two mutually exclusive things at the same time. Perhaps you claim not to want to be in an unhappy relationship, but it turns out that there are lots of things about it that suit you very well.

Lacanians are generally typified by two features—they're interested in language and they give variable length sessions. Jacques Lacan was a French psychiatrist and psychoanalyst who refused to let the clock dictate the length of an appointment. Instead, he would "punctuate" his patients' sessions, stopping at surprising or significant moments. This, he claimed, was a good idea for a number of reasons. It stopped patients trying to control the block of time by rehearsing in advance or making the session into a sort of ritual. This ostensibly meant that more unpredictable unconscious material could emerge. There was also evidence to show that interrupted activities stuck in the mind more than tasks that had been completed. Like a half-watched film, a suddenly finished session might leave questions hanging rather than tying them all up neatly at the end. This could give the work a potency that would lead to more interesting thoughts between appointments.

In spite of all Lacan's claims in support of the variable length session, certain members of the psychoanalytic community felt that the classical "fifty-minute hour" was fundamentally necessary to psychoanalytic treatment—and that Lacan was simply giving short sessions in order to make more money. In response to this came his argument that the standard length of an appointment was just a convention that had sprung up in the scramble to make psychoanalysis into some kind of formalized, respectable practice in the wake of Freud's new and shocking theories. There was nothing sacred about that particular quantity of time. (And there's also the fact that non-clock-watching sessions might sometimes be *longer* than fifty minutes— although this seems to be rare.) The two sides failed to reach an agreement.

Lacan became hugely influential in the fields of philosophy, literary theory, film studies, and feminism. His clinical ideas, too, have spread around the world, but have sometimes been treated with suspicion by people who would prefer to see psychoanalysis practised according to tighter conventions. Nowadays you will find Lacanians who give short sessions and others who don't. It's not the most important feature of Lacanian psychoanalysis, in spite of being the most famous.

As for the second part of the Lacanian caricature—the focus on language—this is also true, while not being quite the whole story. Lacan's conception of the unconscious was far from its being a dark, formless mess. Instead, he depicted it as every bit as codified and organized as the conscious mind, hence his famous statement: "The unconscious is structured like a language." The unconscious was a powerful force that could wreak havoc with your life, but there was nothing pure or animal about it. It was formed in response to a person's entry into language and the symbolic systems that organize human life. It was full of all the things we didn't want to know, but which were constantly pushing for recognition. So the way to access these things would be through speech. The unconscious would articulate itself through slips of the tongue, made-up words, repetitions, metaphors, the forgetting of words, and all manner of other disruptions of language. So while some therapists might encourage their clients to express their rage, own their pain, feel the fear but do it anyway, and so on, Lacanians have a reputation for focussing on linguistic details. For instance, a patient comes in sobbing and howling and says she's leaving her husband, and her analyst asks her to say more about her use of an unusual turn of phrase. While it might sound a bit unsympathetic, the point in an intervention like this might be to cut through the tragic storytelling and to try to access another dimension of the situation. (If that sounds just too horrible, I can only say that my current Lacanian analyst is one of the most considerate people I have ever met. But she does pick me up on words sometimes, even when I'm crying.)

While these sorts of word-centred interpretations really do go on—both here and in other kinds of therapy—there's also another strand of Lacan's work which has to do with dramatization. Lacan was famous for doing peculiar things in sessions—throwing plant pots, speaking in silly voices, and once even dropping his trousers. He argued against the deadening effects of the kind of therapy during which a person might be encouraged to neatly package up their life and try to make sense of it all so that they can walk off into the sunset feeling like they know everything and are therefore OK. Instead, he opened up the possibility of a kind of work where people could be perplexed by unanswerable questions and become more aware of the fact that they aren't entirely in charge of their own minds. In order to do this, he might act out or say strange things so that the patient could be startled out of their habitual ways of perceiving things.

Which leads on to the goal of this sort of analysis. If there was a spectrum of talking treatments with fast cures that stop up the symptom at one end and slower, more investigative treatments at the other, then Lacanian analysis would probably be at the end of the line. Lacan came up with the term "subjective destitution" to describe a state where one had let go of all ideals and narcissistic identifications and become a piece of senseless stuff in a meaningless universe. This would be the ultimate goal of analysis. Of course, at that point, you wouldn't be kicked out onto the street. From a point of having truly inhabited that shocking reality, you may then want to speak about the terms under which you might carry on living. You certainly needn't run into the wilderness and grow a beard down to your knees. You can become a famous actor or go and work in a shoe shop. Whatever you do, it will be in the knowledge that you are just a piece of nothingy something, not a "good", "whole", or "healthy" individual. It's not a happy ending in the conventional sense, but there may be a great deal of relief in it. It may leave a person freer to stop trying to be marvellous and to follow their senseless desires.

Still, the majority of analyses don't reach this point. What's far more normal is that people stop coming, either because they fall in love, get a job in a different country, suddenly take against their shrink, or feel much better and decide to invest the money in holidays. And who's to say they're wrong?

Relational psychoanalysis

Relational psychoanalysis is the term for a recent set of developments in psychoanalytic theory and practice. It's a very post-modern approach to analytic work, informed by critical theory and feminism. Not only is it a collection of ideas that's still very much in progress, but central to relational thinking (if that's not an oxymoron) is the notion that "truth" and "objectivity" are fictions. It's the opposite of a totalizing theory, which presumably means that it will continue to mutate and transform for as long as it can be said to exist.

Relational analysts reject Freud's theory of the drives. Instead of saying that human beings are driven by the impulses to eat, fuck, and destroy, there is the notion that our exchanges with the world outside are the main things that motivate us. (For Freud, the world inside—the forces at work in our own bodies—is primary.) From the minute we are born, it seems, we are inclined to interact. These early relations are central to the construction of the human psyche—by engaging with the external world, we become human ourselves. In this sense, relational analysis follows on from Klein and object relations theory. These first relationships, particularly with our mothers or primary carers, are seen to have an enormous impact on our subsequent perceptions of reality. But while the Freudian concept of the drives is still very important in object relations theory, relationists argue that the drives can't be seen as the baseline—the original source of everything— because they can't be untangled from the world in which they are experienced. Hunger can't be separated from the response to it. If we cry and our mother feeds us, that's one thing. But if she doesn't, that's another. And if we stop crying because we know there'll be no response, that's another thing again. In this sense, it can be argued, we experience *everything*—even our own bodies—in the context of a relationship.

Another place where relationists seriously differ from Kleinians is in the way the exchange with the analyst is managed in sessions. Like humanists, relational psychoanalysts claim no position of authority. They are there to relate, not to impose. They wouldn't systematically assert their views on what's happening in the transference (as in the case of the "flower" interpretation). The idea isn't to interpret or to present the patient with unconscious material. Nor is it to present a blank screen onto which a patient can project their fantasies. The problem with the latter, for a relationist, is that the analyst's blankness can, in itself, transform them into an authoritative presence. A silent analyst may appear constantly implacable, as if they have no troubles or passions of their own. When this is combined with the odd I-know-your-unconscious-better-than-you-do intervention, the analyst can stop seeming like a regular being and become an extremely powerful presence. The patient is a snivelling, complaining, faulty person, while the analyst is an all-knowing ball of serenity. It doesn't exactly make for a non-hierarchical relationship.

To counter the possibility of this sort of extreme power imbalance, relational analysts might sometimes put themselves in question in a session. They would never leave a patient believing (as many people seem inclined to) that everything their analyst says or does is for an extremely good theoretical reason. Maybe sometimes analysts make mistakes, or say the "wrong" thing, in which case this can be discussed with the patient. Relationists also allow for a certain level of self-disclosure—it's OK if the patient knows that their analyst too has experienced unhappiness, confusion, or anxiety. Analysts of this sort may very well write or give talks during which they speak about events in their own lives. They see it as far more important to be human and authentic than to be deadpan and impeccable.

Relational psychoanalysts privilege creativity and surprise over objectivity and authority. The analytic set-up is a two-sided relationship, the dynamics of which are up for discussion. "Mentalization" is an important concept for relationists. It has to do with understanding your own and other people's mental states. Mutual recognition is the key to workable relationships. It's all about intersubjectivity—not subject/object relations. Through a carefully handled, honest relationship with your analyst, the idea is that you should be able to work your way towards more nuanced interactions with other people.

Some practitioners in this field may call themselves psychotherapists rather than psychoanalysts. This could be for any number of reasons, all of which they should be able to give you. It may be to do with the nature of their training, or with their theoretical stance concerning Freud. Because it's such a new area, and because it's an intrinsically flexible way of working, the differences between practitioners will be huge. Some relationists have taken up developments in related areas such as neuropsychoanalysis and may do things like arrange the chairs at certain angles in order to stimulate the right hemisphere of the brain (which deals with creativity). Others might have no interest whatsoever in this sort of practice and will be far more focussed on the particularity of the relation between the two of you. In either case, they should be pretty open about why they do the things they do. Any questions you have will be grist for the intersubjective mill.

CHAPTER TWO

Psychiatry versus psychology

In short, a psychiatrist is a medical doctor and is licensed to prescribe drugs. A psychotherapist, psychoanalyst, or counsellor is there to help you think about your life, and to see if there are ways in which you might want to change it. A clinical psychologist might simply diagnose, or they may also work therapeutically. And a psychologist studies human beings, or animals, but isn't necessarily involved in working directly with patients/clients. Anyone might combine two or more of these titles.

In the past, these fields have perhaps been more closely tied together than they are today. In the early days of psychoanalysis, for instance, it was generally expected that you would first need to be a medical doctor in order to become an analyst. Freud himself argued against this, basically saying that being a doctor didn't necessarily provide you with any insight into the human condition. Still, there continued to be much debate as to whether non-doctors ought to be allowed to train. Until quite recently in America, you had to be a medical doctor if you wanted to be an analyst, but in

Europe this was never the case. Melanie Klein, one of the most influential post-Freudians, was not only not a doctor, but didn't have any kind of university degree at all. This, however, is extremely unusual. Lots of people become psychotherapists after studying psychology—it's just not the only route. A background in the humanities is deemed more appropriate by many training institutes who, like Freud, see an interest in art and literature as a very good starting point for the study of the human psyche. Plenty of actors and performers also train—they are probably quite used to thinking about what it's like to be other people. And they may also be very good at playing the role of a shrink, maybe appearing calm and contained even when their own lives are in turmoil.

Apart from the fact that people might train in a number of different areas, it's also true that individual practitioners will have different takes on their own discipline. Plenty of psychiatrists are humane and easy to talk to, while others bark lists of questions, silently consult the Internet, and pack you off with a prescription. (I once met a psychiatrist at a dinner party who said, "Oh, poor you! You have to listen to them!") Among psychotherapists, there will be some who aim to pack every session with therapeutic possibility, hoping you'll go skipping off down the street each week, while others will see "cure" as a hard-won state reached over months or years of painful labour. Equally, plenty of psychoanalysts wish their patients well and would like to see them suffer less, even though the fast riddance of symptoms isn't top of their agenda. Still, if you want to take Prozac, say, then only a psychiatrist or GP will be able to organize this for you. And if you hate the idea of drugs and need to talk, then a therapist, analyst, or counsellor would generally be a better person to go to.

There's also the possibility that you may benefit from both …

Medication or conversation?

There are plenty of arguments to be had about the relative benefits of tablets and talking cures. On the one hand, why spend time and money on therapy if you can just pop a cheap pill that makes you feel better? But then again, isn't it terrible that some doctors seem to think that all forms of human unhappiness can be placated with drugs? Do drugs help people, or shut them up? And does therapy make people better, or does it simply encourage self-pity and complaining?

Of course, those sorts of polarized arguments tend to over-simplify the situation. In cases of severe psychosis, drugs can save not only the patient's life, but possibly also the lives of people around them. And therapy can *stop* people seeing themselves as hard-done-by victims. It may not even necessarily be a question of one or the other—sometimes a course of antidepressants can stabilize someone so that they can get on with doing some therapeutic work. And going into therapy might gradually help someone drop their reliance on psychiatric drugs; having got yourself out of a crisis with medication, you might then want to find out what's underneath your depression/anxiety/delusion in the hope that you can stop it coming back.

All this, of course, assumes that you actually believe that your current life events and personal history have anything to do with the way you are feeling. Plenty of people aren't convinced by this at all. It's common enough these days for people to see human unhappiness as the result of chemical imbalances in the brain. Maybe some people are genetically prone to certain forms of psychological suffering. There is nothing they can do about the type of brain functioning they've been born with—apart from supplement it with chemicals. Those people are welcome to their opinion if it helps them get through the day, but, in spite of appearing highly scientific, it isn't necessarily altogether logical. While it may be the case that there are people, say, who simply can't synthesize enough serotonin, it's also true that life events have an impact on the body's production of certain chemicals. It's unlikely that *all* the unhappy people in the world are simply beholden to a biological deficiency that could be fixed with a quick supplement. What's far more likely is that they are responding to things that have happened. Hence the end of a love affair can trigger a depression with tangible effects on the brain, as can the beginning of one. And one of the traditional human responses to difficult things happening has been to try to articulate something about it, whether through speech or some other form of expression, like singing or writing. The invention of Prozac is unlikely to do away with this need—as you can see from Elizabeth Wurtzel's excellent book, *Prozac Nation*. In spite of feeling much better, she still felt compelled to write about her experiences. (Another traditional response is to drink alcohol or take recreational drugs—both forms of self-medication—but these tricks also tend not to do away with the need for speaking. Drunks very often like an audience.)

Serotonin is particularly linked to the organism's interactions with the wider world. Four-fifths of the body's serotonin is found in the gut, where it helps to regulate digestion. The rest is processed by the brain. In animals, it's connected with making judgements about how much food there is around. If there's lots of food and potential mates, that's good—you have a happy animal, brimming with serotonin. But it's slightly more complicated than that. The more food the animal finds, the healthier it becomes, and the better it gets at shoving weaker animals out of the way. All that food and synthesized serotonin are giving it the impression that it's a top animal. In experiments, you can see that weedier specimens, when injected with serotonin, suddenly start acting all Alpha. The chemical makes them believe that they are well fed and fanciable. This may be great—their added confidence can make it all happen in real life. Or it may get them killed. The experiments tend to be quite short term and don't, so far, tell us about the impact on animal communities of puny, artificially over-confident specimens.

As a human, what you make of all this is obviously up to you. You might say that the best thing to do in that case is to start taking Prozac and get on with elbowing the weaklings out of the way. This may work, until too many of the weaklings catch on. (Or until you work out what better to do with your increased self-confidence.) Or you could say it just goes to show how intimately linked our brain chemistry is to external forces. Therefore you might want to understand how these forces are impacting on you. And then you might want to think about what you can do about it. If you'd rather avoid the kind of sci-fi scenarios you see described by Aldous Huxley and Philip K. Dick—where people take pills in order to manufacture certain feelings—then this might be an honourable approach. If you can put up with a bit of unhappiness, you may be making the world a better place. But then again, if a course of medication gets you out of bed and perhaps enables you to look after your children—and/or yourself—it might be a very helpful thing.

In terms of proof of effectiveness, neither drugs nor therapy can be said to be demonstrably better. Some studies have claimed that antidepressants work in ninety per cent of cases. But then when you look into it further, you discover that these are the studies that the drug companies want to publish. There are other unpublished studies that cut that figure in half. But more importantly, the very idea of "proof of effectiveness" is very problematic in this context. What if something works brilliantly for one person in twenty? Does that mean it's ineffective? Or just more difficult to market? Statistic-producing questionnaires don't give you access to another person's reality. They have very little to say about complex, individual responses. Studies of both drug and therapy outcomes are largely meaningless because the terms on which they're based are often quite nonsensical. There's no universal agreement as to what constitutes a "good outcome". Therapy is especially hard to assess if you take seriously Freud's idea that analysis can stop you being neurotic so you can get on with being miserable. Is that the sort of success you can measure with a questionnaire? While research into therapeutic outcomes regularly tells us that all forms of therapy are marvellous, it's hard to imagine what this marvellousness actually entails. So if both drugs and therapy ostensibly "work", it just seems to boil down to trial and error or personal preference.

Therapy and psychosis

Perhaps one area where you might hope to find a bit more clarity is in the treatment of psychotic disorders. There are some amazing new drugs, like risperidone, that can be used to treat even severe schizophrenias without zonking the person out, leaving them free to carry on with their work and lives. But this doesn't mean that therapy is therefore unnecessary or useless. Apart from the fact that there are people who really don't want to take drugs, there are also people who find it incredibly helpful to speak to someone even after their more florid symptoms have died down. And there are also people who don't object to taking medication, but who find that it doesn't suit them in practice—even the newest and best drugs leave them feeling strange and out of synch. Up to two-thirds of people who are pre-scribed antipsychotics find that they don't want to take them long term.

Traditionally, there has existed the idea that psy-chotherapy is for people who are simply confused and unhappy, not for people who are schizophrenic or chronically paranoid. While it may be true that these serious illnesses are unlikely to be cured by a quick chat, that doesn't mean you have to go the other way and simply drug people and kick them out before they say anything too weird or difficult.

Psychotherapy with neurotic people generally has a slightly different aim to psychotherapy with psychotic people, although it basically involves discussing many of the same sorts of subjects. In both instances, you might talk about childhood, dreams, relationships, and fantasies, but the therapist would be trying to draw out different things. With neurotic people, you might hope to guide them towards articulating the repressed ideas underlying their symptoms—which can be quite a destabilizing experience. But with a psychotic person, the idea might be to help stabilize them by letting them build and restructure their ideas in such a way as to pin their world in place a bit better. Maybe you would encourage their identification with an admirable person.

Or show support for their art or writing. Or possibly even back up their born-again Christian evangelism. Whatever it is that seems to provide a defence against psychic meltdown. What you wouldn't do is try to show them that they aren't in control of their own minds—as you might with a neurotic.

However, psychotic people are notorious for their intelligence, and for seeing through bullshit, so they may very well have ideas of their own about how a therapy should be conducted. They may have a great interest in the unconscious, and in all the difficult repressed ideas that so many people seem to want to run away from. So while, as a therapist, you might think that psychotic people need one thing and neurotic people another, what you will often find in practice is that everyone is quite insistent on doing it their own way. Neurotics may find excellent stabilizing mechanisms and psychotics might gain a lot from dredging up infantile sexual material. And both may do it with or without drugs.

Of course, all this refers to psychodynamic psychotherapies. CBT and other brief therapies have also been developed for use with psychotic people. In these instances, there may not be such a marked difference of aim. Because with these sorts of treatments the emphasis is generally on stabilization, the diagnosis needn't have too enormous an effect on the methods used in sessions. In either case, you will be given a number of techniques to control and subdue your symptoms. Psychiatrists very often recommend a combination of drugs and CBT. Some of them even recommend this quite forcefully, as if no other forms of treatment are appropriate to psychosis. This is very much a matter of opinion, and plenty of analysts, therapists, and more open-minded psychiatrists argue otherwise, as do many patients—especially those who've experienced the mental health system at first hand.

Which drugs?

There are far too many psychiatric drugs to talk about in detail here, so I'll keep it brief and stick to the most commonly prescribed. These can loosely be divided into two groups: antipsychotics and antidepressants. Still, it's not so straightforward. Antipsychotics are sometimes prescribed to non-psychotic patients, and antidepressants may be used to treat obsessive-compulsive disorder, bulimia, and panic attacks, even when the person isn't at all depressed. Within each group, there are subgroups: typical and atypical antipsychotics; and tricyclic antidepressants (old-fashioned) and selective serotonin reuptake inhibitors, or SSRIs (modern and very popular). There are also much older drugs like lithium, which is still commonly used for the treatment of mania—especially in bipolar disorder.

Antipsychotics (or neuroleptics)

These drugs are mainly used to treat symptoms such as delusions, hallucinations, and disordered thinking, that is, the symptoms of schizophrenia and paranoid psychosis. They were discovered in the 1950s, largely by mistake. The first antipsychotic drugs (typical antipsychotics) were basically anaesthetics, used in low doses to subdue the patient without actually knocking them out. They were often used in place of lobotomies, and perhaps seemed more humane because at least the effects were reversible. Still, they were basically chemical lobotomies, leaving people in a stupor. Books like *One Flew Over the Cuckoo's Nest* focus on the dehumanizing effects of these sorts of tranquillizing drugs. Instead of making people better, they simply floored them so they could be more easily contained. Of course, if you have a huge, violent killer on your hands, you may have to think carefully about how best to handle them, but the risk with these sorts of drugs was that they could be used on anybody who seemed a bit odd or excitable in order to shut them up.

Early antipsychotics had quite serious side effects such as diabetes, muscle spasms, depleted immune system, and sexual dysfunction. They also considerably decreased a person's life expectancy. And this was all aside from the fact that they turned you into a zombie. Plus, they tended to stop working after a while when the body had found ways to overcome them, meaning that the psychosis might return more fiercely than before.

Atypical antipsychotics (risperidone, clozapine, ziprasidone, quetiapine, aripiprazole) began to be developed in the 1990s. They had fewer side effects and didn't totally flatten the person, so people taking them would often be able to carry on with their lives. Still, they sometimes leave people feeling a bit dull. While you can get up and cook a meal and go to work, you may notice that you can't enjoy the world in quite the same way. It's hard to get excited about anything—not nature, not art, not sex—and while everything continues as normal, it's as if there's something seriously missing. This is one of the main reasons that so many people stop taking these drugs after a while. Antipsychotics can make it impossible for people to enjoy even their own private thoughts. Because psychotic people are often extremely thoughtful, this loss can prove too much to bear. Still, for the remaining thirty or so per cent, these drugs may be a life-saver, and they are a great, great improvement on so many of the treatments for madness we have seen over the centuries.

As well as being prescribed for psychotic disorders, these sorts of drugs may also be given to people with Tourette's syndrome, autism, obsessive-compulsive disorder, mood swings, depression, anxiety, and insomnia.

Antidepressants

In the 1950s, depressed people were commonly pre-scribed opioids and amphetamines—basically heroin and speed. Both of these drugs were addictive and could make people behave quite strangely, as well as having a number of unpleasant side effects. There were also tricyclic antidepressants, which were initially a form of synthetic antihistamine which just happened to affect patients' states of mind. They came to be used as both antipsychotic and antidepressant drugs and are still prescribed today. They are seen as being as effective as many of the newer drugs, but have the disadvantage of being lethal in the case of overdose— which Prozac isn't.

The first SSRIs (selective serotonin reuptake inhibi-tors) were made available in the 1980s. Prozac was the famous trade name of the drug fluoxetine, and was seen as a huge leap forward in the medical treatment of depression. Other well-known SSRIs include cita-lopram (Cipramil) and paroxetine (Paxil). It had been discovered that serotonin, a naturally occurring neuro-transmitter, had an effect on a person's sense of well-being. So the theory was developed that if you could make the serotonin hang around in the synapses a bit longer (rather than being snatched away too quickly in a process known as "reuptake"), then the person would feel happier.

During the 1980s and 1990s, huge claims were made on behalf of Prozac and its sister drugs—if you believed what you read in the newspapers, it might have seemed that no one ever need feel unhappy again. But then again, there was a large amount of research that claimed to show that Prozac was only about two per cent more effective than a placebo. Either it cured everything, or it barely worked at all. There were also legal cases around people killing themselves, or other people, while on Prozac. In London, apparently, so many people were taking it that there were traces of it in the tap water. It was the best and worst of drugs.

Since then, perhaps, the excitement around it has died down. Some people find it works brilliantly, others find it impossible, with side effects that include vomiting, dizziness, loss of appetite, insomnia, anxiety, suicidal thoughts, and, perhaps most commonly, a loss of sexual desire. Newer developments include drugs that go to work on other neurotransmitters (norepinephrine and dopamine) at the same time. In some instances, these can reduce side effects, and they may be more effective in cases of chronic depression.

If you feel that these sorts of drugs may help you, it's often a question of trying a few different ones, under the supervision of your GP or psychiatrist, and seeing what works best. Everyone seems to respond differently to the different brands and to different doses. Because these drugs can take a few weeks to become effective, you may need to be quite patient in the process of finding the right one. And if you decide that they really aren't for you, always remember that they aren't compulsory, however religiously some doctors seem to believe in them.

CHAPTER THREE

Individuals, groups, couples, and children

Couples and families

Given that your problems are unlikely to be totally discrete and independent from the people around you, might it make more sense to all go into therapy together? If you are having trouble with your relationship, for example, then perhaps it would be wise to go and see someone as a couple. This, may be easier said than done. Whether you go into therapy by yourself or with one or more significant people might depend first of all on whether those other people agree that therapy is a good idea. You often hear about wives who want their husbands to go to marriage guidance counselling but who just can't persuade them to do it—either because the husbands can't see what the problem is, or because they want to leave without talking about it first. You can't make someone go into therapy, however much you think they need to, so this sort of campaign is very often doomed. If this is your case, the best thing might be to ask yourself why you want to go. Do you want your errant spouse to be told off by a professional in front of you? Do you want to have your relationship problems solved by someone who knows best? Or do you want to try to understand the situation a bit better in order to see how it might be handled differently? If it's the last one, then it may be just as worthwhile to go it alone. Even if it really is true that the other person is doing things that make life together impossible—taking loads of drugs, hitting you, or never coming home—it may be worth asking yourself a few difficult questions about what's keeping you there. Couples counselling, even when both parties regularly turn up willingly, isn't a magic bullet. Rather than helping people live joyously into old age together, it might just as often help them to split up.

Going into therapy as a family, or any other kind of group, is a very interesting, risky business. The therapist won't simply be there for you, but will have to take everyone's point of view equally seriously. You may have to deal with the possibility of their being extremely sympathetic to someone who drives you nuts. But of course this is an essential part of the process. If you go into therapy with one or more other people, you will almost inevitably be invited to see things from their perspective. And they will, with luck, try to see things from yours. Quite often, the therapy itself is a battle to win the therapist's approval, but in this process lots of things are bound to be exposed. If some people fight for attention while others sit and glower in the hope of being noticed, then the therapist will perhaps be able to deduce important things from all of this.

As with couples counselling, the end result of family therapy needn't be a *Waltons*-style love-in. It may even turn out that the idea that everyone *should* love each other is part of the problem. Perhaps the differences between you would be less painful if you didn't feel obliged to spend all your Sundays and holidays together. Rather than bringing you all together, the therapy may encourage you to spend more time apart. Therapy in pairs or groups is always going to be a bit of an experiment—and sometimes a more volatile experiment than one-to-one work due to the greater conflict of interests. It may turn out that one person gets a great deal out of it and another person thinks it's rubbish. And the "winner" may not always be the one who wanted to go in the first place ...

Like one-to-one therapy, group, family, and couples therapy loosely falls into two camps. There are the people who are more interested in surface phenomena (cognitive and behavioural therapists) and the ones who are more interested in what might be going on beneath the surface (the psychodynamic people). Which you choose would depend on what seems to suit everyone better—although it may well be that you even have different ideas about this. Some of you might prefer to be given a few useful tips and strategies for dealing with one another, while the rest would like to rip off façades and find out what's *really* going on between the lot of you. But at least an argument about different approaches to therapy might make a refreshing break from the norm.

Group therapy

Apart from family and couples counselling, there's also the option of going into therapy with a bunch of strangers. This seems to be particularly popular in organizations like the NHS—perhaps because you can supposedly get a job lot done for the price of one. Still, group therapy is far from simply being a cut-price version of the real thing. It can be incredibly fascinating—and hard. Not only do you have to find ways to say the things you need to say, you also have to do it in front of a load of other people, and to listen and respond to them too. It can be a dramatic way to shift the focus away from yourself and your problems and to think more broadly about the sorts of things people have to face in their lives. It can also teach you a lot about the ways in which the things you do affect other people. You might think that by being quiet and polite you can minimize your effect on people and pass through life unnoticed. And then someone in therapy will tell you that they find your Miss Perfect act absolutely nauseating and that they wish you'd let yourself slip up once in a while. Or you may imagine that by being jovial and light-hearted you cheer other people up. But then you find that your blustering chirpiness makes them feel like they can't say anything real or serious around you.

These sorts of revelations can be shocking—plus, there's the possibility that you needn't take them too seriously. The other people in the group have *their* problems, after all, and maybe these are affecting their perceptions of you. So should you dig and find out what makes you so annoyingly chipper? Should you learn to block out criticism better? Or should you try to understand what would make that particular person say that? Maybe you could even end up having a go at all three. Whatever you do, it will hopefully be a worthwhile foray into the complexities of coexistence.

It would be impossible to say whether group or individual therapy is better. Plenty of people do both— sometimes running simultaneously. (Especially people in prisons or hospitals who may have time on their side, access to free treatment, and a strong incentive to sort something out.) It may be harder to look into personal material in any great detail in group therapy—depending on how often you meet and how many people go. The fact that everyone will need a turn, and that whatever they say may very well affect what you say, means it can sometimes be a bit of a battle to articulate the things you feel you need to. But if, in the process, you find yourself thinking seriously about how to negotiate your own needs in relation to those around you, then perhaps you're already halfway there.

Child psychology

This is becoming more common in schools. Pupils who are having trouble with anything from schoolwork to friendship might be offered sessions with a child psychologist. These people interact with the child through speaking, playing, and possibly drawing or painting. They may very well liaise with the child's carers, but they would also preserve a space for the child to be able to speak freely without fear of getting into trouble with parents or teachers.

Child psychologists can't prescribe drugs, but they may be able to diagnose a number of disorders such as attention deficit hyperactivity disorder (ADHD) or autism. If your child seems to be suffering from something more intractable than a transient period of frustration or unhappiness, a psychologist should be able to advise you about possible courses of action. However, one of the most helpful things might be for the child to carry on talking to someone. If a child is acting up or suffering as a result of the things going on around them, a psychologist will try to help them understand their own feelings a bit better—and perhaps also the feelings of other people. Much of the psychology practised in schools is very child-led. The focus isn't on tests and questionnaires, but on letting the child find ways to express him- or herself.

Because this sort of thing has become so commonplace, there often seems to be little or no stigma attached. Becoming human, living in a family, and going to school are potentially all already quite difficult—and that's before your parents split up, become ill, or lose their jobs. It's not so strange that some children develop odd symptoms to help get themselves through difficult moments. Maybe they start bedwetting, or stop eating, or hit another child. While it would be nice if they could sail through childhood without putting a foot wrong, invariably they don't—and odd behaviours or symptoms tend to signal that there is something going on that they don't know quite how to process.

If you have a child who's really struggling, you may even want to go into therapy together—especially if there's something tangible in the way you relate that seems to be causing problems. Maybe they fight with you or cling to you or ignore you. It's possible that a family therapist might be able to help you find ways to get along better, and to help you to understand each other. But it's also possible that it would be a good idea to see someone separately. Not only can it be extremely draining to have a child who's having a hard time, it may also be difficult to be frank in front of them. Perhaps a relation to a step-parent is a factor in the situation, say, and it would be inappropriate to discuss the nuts and bolts of the relationship with your child there. Or maybe things are difficult with their other biological parent. If you have the sense that things in your own life might be impacting on your child's life, it mightn't be such a bad idea to look into the whole business separately. That way, your child will have a chance to explore a few ideas independently, and you may find you can get to the heart of things better without the constraint of having to keep the discussions child-friendly.

CHAPTER FOUR

Finding a therapist

Having decided you'd like to go and speak to someone, the next question is how to track them down. One of the first decisions you'll have to make is whether to find someone independently, or go through your doctor. There are advantages and disadvantages to each. Perhaps one of the key factors in the decision would be how much you like and trust your doctor. If they're sympathetic and easy to talk to, then it might very well be worth sounding them out about seeing a therapist. If you are in the UK, or any other country with a state-funded health service, they should be able to find you someone to speak to within the NHS, or they may be able to offer you the contact details of private practitioners whom they know or have somehow vetted. The very serious downside of seeing an NHS therapist is that you may have to wait for as long as two years before your first appointment. There's also the fact that you might have little or no say about what type of therapist you see, or how long you see them for. On the upside, you won't have to pay.

In America, and other countries without a free health service, your doctor may be able to point you in the direction of a therapist who promises to suit both you and your insurance company. Here too, you may find your choices are quite restricted as to the type of treatment and number of sessions—it would depend on the level of health insurance you have.

Wherever you are, there is also the possibility that your doctor will have their own strong opinions about therapy—and that these won't chime with yours. Some doctors think therapy is a waste of time and that drugs are far more effective. Others may have great faith in some forms of therapy and none whatsoever in others. A GP needn't be any kind of specialist in the field of talking cures—they may know little or nothing about the arguments for and against different kinds of therapy. So while they ought to be able to provide you with a phone number or two, there's no reason to assume that their advice is any more authoritative than that of a trusted friend.

To pay or not to pay?

If you have absolutely no spare cash, then this is an easy one to answer. But even if you have only a very small amount to spend on therapy, it may be worth looking into seeing someone privately. Lots of therapy organizations offer low-cost appointments. These may sometimes be with trainees, but they may also be with experienced therapists who have a civic conscience and keep some places aside for low-cost work. And then, of course, there's always the question of which is better. A trainee may be someone who has a great deal of experience in a related area. They could be a counsellor or social worker who is retraining as a psychotherapist—and whoever they are, they will be in supervision with someone who's been practising for a lot longer. So the low-cost route certainly doesn't suggest a bargain-basement, dodgy option. Even if you were given someone new to the work, they may be brilliant at it. Most therapists remember their first cases very strongly and speak about the strange intensity of those early encounters. It may be the therapist's very inexperience that makes them more conscientious and curious.

If you choose this route, the way to do it would be to find out which organizations offer a low-cost service. You should be able to do this either online or through a therapy association registered with an umbrella organisation like the United Kingdom Council for Psychotherapy or the American Therapy Association. Once you have found a group who provide therapy for a lower fee, you will then generally be invited in for an assessment with a fully qualified practitioner. They will talk with you about your circumstances and your reasons for seeking therapy. If it seems appropriate, they will then refer you on to an available therapist.

It's possible that your case will be deemed unsuitable for a trainee. If this is so, you will then either be referred to someone more experienced who is prepared to take on low-cost clients, or they may suggest you look for another form of treatment. The reasons for this may be anything from the idea that you are too wily to be handed over to someone fresh to the field, or that something about your situation is too upsetting or risky. (If someone is feeling seriously suicidal, for instance, it may not be a good idea for them to work with a trainee—as much for the trainee's sake as for theirs.) If this happens, and if you think that private low-cost work is the only kind that will do for you, you needn't give up. Different organizations will have varying numbers of experienced and available therapists. You may fare differently if you try your luck elsewhere. It can sometimes take a little bit of time to find someone within reach, whom you like, and who is prepared to work with you for below the market rate. But as long as you don't expect to sort it out in a hurry, it ought to be possible somehow.

If money isn't top of your list of worries, then you will certainly be able to see someone sooner—and for longer if you need/want to—if you are prepared to pay for your therapy yourself. Apart from speeding up the process, another very great advantage of paying is that it may push you to make the sessions more fruitful. (This would apply to paying a lower fee too—£10 to you may be the equivalent to £100 to someone else.) Speaking as someone who has seen both NHS and private therapists, and who has worked in a state-funded clinic as well as privately, it's not hard to see that an exchange of cash can make a great difference to the work. If you're financing it yourself, you probably won't want to be wasting your time there.

However, one of the difficulties of paying is that it can sometimes become the focus of complicated feelings. You may wonder whether your therapist really gives a damn about you or is only seeing you for the money. You may sometimes feel that they offer you less in the way of valuable advice than most of your unpaid friends. And if you want to stop your therapy and your therapist tries to persuade you otherwise, you may suspect them of being driven by financial incentives rather than by your best interests.

Speaking to someone in a therapeutic/analytic setting is quite different to speaking to someone anywhere else, and the fact that the therapist gets paid is obviously one of the things that makes this the case. But if you wanted to meet regularly with a friend and tell them whatever was on your mind, you'd still have to offer them *something*. Either you'd have to be very entertaining or charming, or you'd have to cook for them and/or listen to their problems in return. If you failed to do any one of those things, you might find that the person wasn't available the following week. You might not even know what you are giving the other person—so if they suddenly disappeared or became upset with you, it would be very hard to understand why. And even if they saw you long term for no apparent reason, you might feel you were incurring some kind of debt to them. Paying for therapy means you don't have to feel indebted or crushingly grateful to your therapist for trying to help you. It also means that *you* can end the relationship at any time without feeling like a scoundrel.

The fee you pay your therapist is one of the things that ensures they will be there for you, no matter how unhappy, frustrated, or conversationally one-sided you are. (Of course this doesn't mean you can seriously mistreat them—harassing or threatening a therapist is a crime.) It's a fixed amount of money, and not some mysterious quality or function that you somehow seem to fulfil for them. You don't *have* to make your therapist love you (although you may find that you want to) because that's not the primary reason why they sit there and listen to you week after week. This should mean that you can explore the tricks and strategies you have for dealing with other people, rather than simply acting them out *again*. If you are anxious that people won't like you if you stop putting on your usual act, then therapy might be the one place you can afford to experiment with letting your guard down. So the fee not only means that *you* may have a stronger incentive to do some work, it also means that your therapist will have a concrete reason to put themselves out for you and do some work too. If one day you get angry with them, or simply sit there in silence, they won't sulk and refuse to speak to you for a month, but will see your feelings or actions as an intrinsic part of your joint project.

Of course, it would be simplistic to say that the money being exchanged means that everything's therefore perfectly clear and straightforward. You might ask why anyone would *want* to be a therapist, rather than getting money from working with nice things like flowers or pastries. What do they get out of it? Are they a saint or a sadist? And which is worse? (Perhaps you don't fret over why a chef has provided you with a meal—although the forces in his life that led him to be doing that may be very strange indeed.) It may still be true that you worry a great deal about what your therapist thinks of you, or why they have chosen to make themselves the witness of so much unhappiness, but the fact that they need to eat and pay heating bills can, at least in part, answer these questions for you.

All this, of course, would go for an insurance- or state-funded therapist too. The only difference here would be in the case of cancellations. It's common practice for private therapists to charge for skipped sessions. If they are working at a state-funded clinic and being paid a wage, then it may not matter so much to you or to them whether you turn up for all your appointments. But if they are working for themselves and have given one of their appointment slots to someone who regularly doesn't show up, then it may matter more. By charging people for missed appointments, they may not only be making their own work viable, they are also creating a situation where it's more annoying for the client to cancel than to show up. Given that therapy is quite an odd business—you may not feel it's worth going on days when you feel happy, or you might feel guilty about investing time and money in yourself at all—there will always be more or less legitimate reasons to cancel. Perhaps you have a headache *because* of your looming appointment, not in spite of it. So in private work you may find yourself far more obliged to show up for your sessions than in work where there's nothing much lost if you choose instead to spend your free hour in bed or at the park.

Having said that, you'd hope that most private therapists apply this practice with judgement. There are terrible urban myths about grieving families being sent invoices by the dead person's shrink. In the field of payments, as in all other areas of the work, you can expect a good therapist to exhibit some tact.

Finding a therapist independently

Perhaps the best and easiest way to find a therapist is by personal recommendation. If a friend tells you they know someone or, better, have been to see someone they thought was good, ask for their number and ring them up. Even if they don't have spaces themselves, they may be able to give you some numbers of individuals or organizations to try.

If you don't have the good fortune to know someone who knows someone, the next best thing might be the Internet. But if the idea of going to see some randomly selected person, possibly alone in their house, seems like a bad idea, you can always go through a larger therapy organization. If any of the schools of thought in the earlier chapters seemed appealing, you could Google the word and find an institute dealing with that particular form of therapy. Alternatively, you could go through one of the larger accreditation bodies, many of which have websites where you can locate therapists according to their orientation and/or postcode. This way, you will at least know that the therapist is somehow linked in with other people. On many individual therapists' websites, they will mention their accreditation body, so you can always double check on them if you want to.

If, during your searches, you come across somebody who sounds good, then get in touch with them to set up an appointment. If you find it hard to tell who's good, or who might suit you, it wouldn't be unusual to set up a few appointments with different people to see who you like best. Some therapists offer these initial conversations for free and some don't. If they are particularly busy, they may not be able to spare time for vaguely curious people and may charge for initial consultations in order to weed out the time-wasters from the serious people. So if you want to check out five therapists, it may prove quite expensive, depending on their policies concerning first appointments.

During a first meeting, it would be impossible to set general rules about what to watch out for. Only you can know what you are looking for in a therapist. All you can do is be intuitive. Does it seem possible to say the things you want to say? Do they respond to you in ways that seem appropriate? Do you feel comfortable enough in their space? Do they inspire respect in you? If they really seem to be wrong for you, don't book a second appointment. It can be quite disorienting to go and speak to a therapist for the first time. You might feel extremely vulnerable and exposed. It can be hard to make judgements about the other person when you are already feeling quite strange in yourself. But if they really leave you with the impression that they can't help you, it may be best to try someone else. And if you're vaguely unsure, you don't have to book your second appointment straight away. Perhaps you need to go home and have a think about this initial conversation. It can be a lot to absorb, and you might want to process what's happened before you take any further steps. Again, a tactful therapist will understand very well how difficult this part of the process can be. They may ask you questions about how you feel about it, or they may just carefully leave you to collect your thoughts and to call them back once you've reached your own conclusions.

When I was in my mid-twenties, I was referred to two women who worked as a pair. They were bossy and coercive and, in spite of having just met me, felt it was within their remit to tell me that I had serious problems—and, by implication, really needed their help. When I said I didn't want to see them, they told me very authoritatively that I couldn't run away from myself that easily. It was easy enough to run away from *them* though, and to find a shrink who actually let me speak. I can't imagine what it might have been like to have bowed down to their authority and submitted myself to years of their headmistress-like domination, but I'm glad I didn't. Still, I can see that someone else might have found their self-assurance extremely confidence-inspiring and gone on to benefit greatly from their stern wisdom. They just weren't for me.

Sometimes it happens that you are simply given a phone number, you see the person, and it's great. But perhaps more often it can take a little bit of time to get it right. Finding a therapist who you want to work with may be a matter of trial and error. Sometimes people try a short treatment first, or do a few months of work with someone and then stop. Maybe then they see, with a bit of distance, that the therapy was actually going somewhere and then resume it again, either with someone else or with the same person.

Of course, if you're going to get any useful work done at all, you will probably have to commit to a certain therapist at some point. Maybe you'll think they're perfect, maybe you won't. Perhaps a useful parallel would be with marriage. There's the question of whether arranged marriages or romantic matches are better. Should you fall madly in love and swear undying devotion? Or does that tend to lead to trouble? Is it better to start off with mixed expectations, with a spouse who's been picked for you? Then you will have to learn how to get along, without the unrealistically high hopes that falling in love can give you. Similarly, is it better to hold out for a shrink who seems to you to be totally perfect? (In which case, they may risk a terrible fall from grace.) Or would it be better for you—and possibly for them—if you saw them as someone perfectly adequate with whom you could try to work something out? Given that finding a therapist isn't the easiest thing in the world—there may be waiting lists, lack of availability in your area (even privately)—there's a lot to be said for giving both them and yourself a chance and seeing what you can do.

It's not unusual for friends and couples in therapy to compete over whose therapist is better. Maybe when you hear about what goes on in your friend's sessions, you wonder why your therapist isn't kinder/sterner/more silent with you. You might ask yourself whether you'd be improving faster with someone else. Have you picked the "right" therapist? The "right" kind of therapy? And then you come up against the undeniable fact that there's really no such thing. Still, the very imperfection of therapy could be said to be one of its strengths. If it doesn't give false promises, but offers a real space in which to address difficult thoughts and feelings, then that's already an extremely valuable thing.